BARBADOS TRAVEL GUIDE 2023-2024

Unveiling The Soul Of Caribbean- The Visitor's Companion To Explore Breathtaking Beaches, Vibrant Culture, And Exotic Flavors

James Robert

COPYRIGHT

All rights reserved. No part of this publication may be reproduced, distributed, or transmitted in any form or by any means, including photocopying, recording, or other electronic or mechanical methods, without the prior written permission of the publisher, except in the case of brief quotations embodied in critical reviews and certain other noncommercial uses permitted by copyright law.

Copyright ©James Robert, 2023.

Table Of Content

INTRODUCTION 7
CHAPTER ONE 11
   Overview History Of The Island 11
   Understanding The Culture And Tradition 14
   Knowing The Geography And Climate 17
   Religion In Barbados 22
   Local Laws And Etiquette 24
CHAPTER TWO 29
   Health And Safety Tips For Visitors 29
   Money Matters And Currency Exchange 31
   Language In Barbados 33
   Communication And Internet Access 35
   Packing Essential List For Visitors 37
CHAPTER THREE 41
   The Perfect Season To Visit Barbados 41
   How To Get There 43
      Visa And Entry Requirements 44
   Getting Around On Arrival 46
      Public Transportation 48
      Car Rental 50
   Accommodation Options 53
      Luxury Hotels And Resorts 54
      Boutique Hotels And Guesthouses 58
      Camping And Eco-Tourism 60

CHAPTER FOUR 65

    Food And Drink In Barbados.. 65

    Local Cuisine And Specialties To Try Out............................... 66

    Barbados Seafood Delicacies... 69

    Best Restaurants And Cafes In Barbados 71

    Bars And Nightlife... 75

    Dinning Etiquette For Visitors.. 77

CHAPTER FIVE 81

    Top Landmarks And Attractions To Visit 81

    Harrison Cave 82

    Nicholas Abbey.. 85

    Bridge Town 87

    Barbados Wildlife Reserve 89

    Beaches And Coastal Areas 91

    Marine Life And Coral Reefs 94

    Caves And Underground Rivers 96

CHAPTER SIX 99

    Off-Road Adventure 99

    Village And Community Tours 100

    Historic Churches To Visit 102

    Museums And Galleries.. 104

    Cultural Festival And Event In Barbados 106

CHAPTER SEVEN 111

    Outdoor Adventure To Try Out 111

    Fishing And Boating 111

    Golfing 113

Scuba Diving And Snorkeling 115
Skydiving And Paragliding 117
Ziplining And Surfing 119
Hiking And Trekking 121
Sustainable Tourism Practices 123
CHAPTER EIGHT **127**
Shopping In Barbados 127
Local Markets And Shopping Malls 129
Souvenirs And Gifts To Buy 132
Essential Websites And Apps For Travelers 134
Travel Agencies And Tour Operators In Barbados 137
Glossary Of Common Bajan Terms For Visitors 139
CONCLUSION **145**
Waving Farewell To The Soul Of The Caribbean 145

INTRODUCTION

Welcome to Barbados, a land of enchantment and wonder, where the sweet melodies of steel drums mingle with the gentle rustle of palm leaves, and the sun-kissed sands carry the echoes of a storied past. Step into a world where adventure meets tranquility, where vibrant culture dances with timeless traditions, and where every moment is an exquisite tapestry of emotions waiting to be unraveled.

Envision yourself strolling along the sunlit beaches, the powdery sands hugging your feet as you gaze out over the vast expanse of the crystalline sea. The waves beckon you to immerse yourself in their embrace, promising unforgettable encounters with a kaleidoscope of marine life beneath the turquoise surface. The warmth of the Caribbean sun upon your skin invites you to let go of your worries and embrace the island's joyful rhythm.

But Barbados is far more than just a picture-perfect postcard destination; it is a treasure trove of history and heritage. This island carries a captivating story etched into every coral stone, every sugar plantation, and every colorful chattel house. As you wander through the ancient streets of Bridgetown, a UNESCO World Heritage site, you'll find yourself journeying back through time to an era of pirates, explorers, and resilient communities that have shaped the island's soul.

Yet, it is not just the island's history that makes Barbados so enthralling. It is the warmth of its people, whose smiles are as bright as the sunshine. Bajans, as the locals are affectionately called, open their hearts and homes to visitors, welcoming them into a tapestry of hospitality, camaraderie, and unity. From the lively celebrations of Crop Over to the soulful harmonies of gospel choirs, every aspect of Barbadian life is infused with a profound sense of community and belonging.

Prepare to embark on an emotional journey of self-discovery as you explore the island's rich cultural heritage. Taste the explosion of flavors in Bajan cuisine, a symphony of sweet and savory that mirrors the island's diverse influences. From flying fish and cou-cou to savory pudding and souse, each dish tells a tale of tradition and a fusion of cultures that have woven Barbados into the vibrant tapestry it is today.

As the sun bids its daily farewell, casting a mesmerizing palette of colors across the sky, find solace in the tranquil beauty of Barbados' landscapes. Wander amidst the mystical caves and towering cliffs of Bathsheba, where the crashing waves seem to sing their own haunting melody. Seek rejuvenation in the lush gardens of Hunte's Gardens, where exotic flora embraces you in a world of lush greenery.

Beyond the beaches and the bustling towns, Barbados invites you to explore its hidden corners, to meet its warm-hearted inhabitants, and to forge unforgettable connections that will stay etched in your heart long after your journey has ended. The island's charm will weave its way into your soul, leaving you forever enchanted by the magic of Barbados.

With an eager heart and an open mind, embark on this extraordinary odyssey through the enchanting shores of Barbados. Let the warmth of its people, the beauty of its landscapes, and the richness of its culture leave an indelible mark on your spirit. Discover the essence of a place where the past and the present unite, where joy knows no boundaries, and where the true meaning of life is etched in every smile.

Welcome to Barbados – a journey of a lifetime awaits you!

CHAPTER ONE

Overview History Of The Island

Barbados, an enchanting Caribbean island nestled in the easternmost part of the Lesser Antilles, has a rich and diverse history that spans over centuries. Its journey from the ancient days of indigenous peoples to a thriving modern nation is a testament to the resilience, adaptability, and cultural fusion that have shaped the island's unique identity.

Early Settlement and Indigenous Peoples:

Long before European explorers set foot on its shores, Barbados was inhabited by Amerindian tribes. The island's first settlers, believed to be the Arawaks, arrived around 1000 AD. They were later followed by the Caribs, who migrated from South America. These indigenous peoples thrived on the fertile land, cultivating crops such as yams, cassava, and corn while fishing and hunting provided additional sustenance.

European Colonization:

The 15th century marked the beginning of Barbados' colonial history when Portuguese and Spanish explorers encountered the island during their voyages. However, it was not until 1625 that the British established a permanent settlement. Captain John Powell, an Englishman, claimed the island for King James I of England and named it 'Los Barbados' after the bearded fig trees he found abundantly growing across the land.

The early years of colonization were challenging, with conflicts between the British settlers and the indigenous Caribs leading to their eventual extinction on the island. Moreover, Barbados initially faced economic difficulties, relying on tobacco cultivation and other ventures that yielded little profit. It wasn't until the introduction of sugar cane in the mid-17th century that the island's fortunes began to change drastically.

The Sugar Revolution and the Age of Plantations:

The 1640s marked a turning point in Barbados' history with the arrival of African slaves, who were brought to the island to work on the burgeoning sugar plantations. The combination of fertile soil, favorable climate, and the labor-intensive cultivation of sugar cane led to an economic boom known as the Sugar Revolution. With the success of sugar as the primary export, Barbados became one of the wealthiest and most important colonies in the British Empire during the 17th and 18th centuries.

However, this prosperity came at a high cost. The brutal and inhumane treatment of enslaved Africans under the plantation system left an indelible mark on the island's history, and the legacy of slavery continues to shape Barbadian society today.

Abolition of Slavery and Emancipation:

The early 19th century witnessed the rise of abolitionist movements, and the British Parliament passed the Slavery Abolition Act in 1833, which provided for the gradual emancipation of slaves throughout the British Empire. In 1834, slavery was officially abolished in Barbados, and thousands of former slaves gained their freedom.

Post-Emancipation Challenges and Social Change:

The post-emancipation period presented significant challenges for the island. With the decline of the plantation economy, Barbados underwent a series of social and economic transformations. Former slaves sought new opportunities and began to acquire small plots of land, giving rise to a small-scale farming system that diversified the island's agricultural output.

As the 20th century dawned, Barbados experienced further changes, with the emergence of a vibrant cultural identity. The blending of African, European, and indigenous influences gave birth to unique art, music, and cuisine. The island's festivals, including Crop Over, became vibrant celebrations of its cultural heritage.

Towards Independence:

Barbados continued to evolve politically, and in 1966, it achieved full independence from British rule. The nation retained a parliamentary system of government, with the British monarch as the ceremonial head of state, represented by a Governor-General. Since independence, Barbados has maintained a stable democratic government, fostering an environment of political and social stability that has contributed to its continued prosperity.

Modern Barbados:

Today, Barbados stands as a beacon of Caribbean success, with a thriving economy driven by tourism, international business, and financial services. The island's pristine beaches, warm climate, and welcoming hospitality attract visitors from all corners of the globe, contributing significantly to its economy.

Barbados has also made remarkable strides in education, healthcare, and infrastructure, establishing itself as a model for other developing nations. The people of Barbados take pride in their cultural heritage and traditions while embracing the challenges of a rapidly changing world.

The history of Barbados is a captivating tale of resilience, transformation, and cultural fusion. From its ancient Amerindian roots to the heights of the sugar era and the struggles of emancipation, the island's journey has been marked by triumphs and tribulations. Today, as an independent nation, Barbados continues to flourish, its history and culture interwoven to create a tapestry of diversity and unity that makes it a truly unique destination in the Caribbean and beyond.

Understanding The Culture And Tradition

Barbados, the jewel of the Caribbean, is not only renowned for its pristine beaches and azure waters but also for its rich and captivating culture that has been shaped by a tapestry of influences from around the world. The island's cultural heritage is a colorful blend of African, European, and indigenous traditions, reflected in its music, dance, cuisine, festivals, and warm hospitality.

Music and Dance:

Music is the heartbeat of Barbados, and its rhythms can be felt resonating through the air wherever you go. One of the most iconic musical genres is calypso, a form of storytelling through song that has its roots in West Africa. Calypso, with its catchy melodies and witty lyrics, often addresses social and political issues with a touch of humor and satire. Another popular musical expression is soca, a fusion of soul and calypso, which dominates the airwaves during the island's vibrant Carnival season.

The pulsating beat of reggae, a genre hailing from neighboring Jamaica, is also embraced by Bajans (Barbadian people) and adds to the island's musical diversity. The local folk music, called spouge, incorporates elements of African rhythms, calypso, and soul, making it distinctly Barbadian.

Accompanying the melodies are the rhythmic movements of traditional dances like the tuk band and the Landship. The tuk band, led by a kettle drum, fife, and penny whistle, exudes energy and charm as dancers display intricate footwork and lively gestures. The Landship dance, on the other hand, originated from a historical association of former slaves imitating British naval officers, and it showcases the pride and spirit of the island's people.

Cuisine:

Barbadian cuisine is a delicious blend of flavors and spices that reflects the island's cultural diversity. At the heart of Bajan cuisine is the reliance on fresh, locally sourced ingredients. Flying fish, the national dish, is a true delicacy, often served with cou-cou, a cornmeal and okra dish. Seafood plays a significant role in Barbadian gastronomy, with dishes like grilled swordfish, blackened tuna, and shrimp cooked in a variety of ways.

The island's vibrant street food scene offers treats like cutters, which are sandwich-like creations filled with fish, pork, or chicken, and pudding and souse, a flavorful combination of pickled pork and sweet potato pudding. Bajans are also fond of indulging in hearty stews and pepperpot, a rich meat and vegetable dish simmered to perfection.

Festivals and Celebrations:

Barbados is a place of joyous celebrations, with numerous festivals throughout the year that showcase the island's culture and traditions. The most famous of these is Crop Over, a vibrant carnival-like festival that dates back to the 18th century. Crop Over originally celebrated the end of the sugar cane harvest, and today it involves colorful parades, calypso competitions, arts and crafts exhibitions, and culinary delights. The festival reaches its climax with the crowning of the Crop Over King and Queen.

Oistins Fish Festival is another much-anticipated event, celebrating the island's fishing heritage with competitions, music, and delectable seafood feasts. The Holetown Festival commemorates the arrival of the first settlers in Holetown in 1627 and features a grand street parade, traditional music, and arts and crafts displays.

Hospitality and Community:

A defining aspect of Barbadian culture is the warm hospitality and strong sense of community that Bajans extend to both locals and visitors alike. Known for their friendly and welcoming nature, Barbadians take pride in making guests feel at home and sharing their culture with open arms.

Community spirit is strong in Barbados, and this is evident in the way people come together to celebrate special occasions, support one another during challenging times, and foster a sense of unity across the island.

Religion and Traditions:

Religion plays a significant role in the lives of many Bajans, with Christianity being the dominant faith. The island is home to numerous churches, some of which have a long history dating back to the colonial era. Religious festivals and ceremonies are an integral part of Barbadian life, bringing together families and communities in moments of devotion and celebration.

Traditional practices, such as fish fries on Friday evenings or rum shops, where locals gather to enjoy the island's famous rum and engage in lively conversations, provide glimpses into the heart of Barbadian daily life and culture.

Preservation and Continuity:

Efforts are made to preserve and promote Barbados' rich cultural heritage. The Barbados Museum and Historical Society, located in a former military prison, houses exhibits that trace the island's history, from pre-colonial times to the present. Various cultural centers and institutions also work tirelessly to showcase traditional arts, crafts, and music, ensuring that the legacy of Barbadian culture continues to thrive.

Knowing The Geography And Climate

Geography

Located in the western part of the Atlantic Ocean, east of the Windward Islands and Saint Vincent and the Grenadines, this coral limestone island is a testament to the beauty and bounty of nature. From its stunning beaches and rolling hills to its rugged cliffs and lush vegetation, Barbados offers a captivating tapestry of geography that enthralls both locals and visitors alike.

Physical Features:

Barbados boasts a compact land area of approximately 166 square miles (430 square kilometers), making it one of the smaller Caribbean islands. Despite its modest size, the island is characterized by a varied topography that lends to its unique charm.

The coastline is undoubtedly one of Barbados' greatest assets, spanning approximately 60 miles (97 kilometers). The western and southern coasts are known for their picturesque beaches, with powdery white sands gently caressed by the crystal-clear waters of the Caribbean Sea. These shores provide ideal conditions for swimming, snorkeling, and water sports, making them popular destinations for tourists seeking sun-soaked bliss.

In contrast, the eastern and northern coasts face the more turbulent waters of the Atlantic Ocean. Here, rugged cliffs, coral formations, and dramatic waves have sculpted the landscape, creating breathtaking vistas and natural wonders such as the Animal Flower Cave, a subterranean cave with mesmerizing rock formations and a natural pool.

Terrain and Interior:

The interior of Barbados is characterized by rolling hills, gently undulating countryside, and fertile plains. The island's highest point, Mount Hillaby, stands at approximately 1,115 feet (340 meters) above sea level and offers panoramic views of the surrounding landscapes. The lush vegetation of the central region is dotted with quaint villages, sugar cane fields, and picturesque plantations, all contributing to the island's distinct rural charm.

Geologically, Barbados is unique among its Caribbean counterparts as it is composed mainly of coral limestone, formed from the accumulation of coral reefs over millions of years. This limestone foundation is responsible for the island's numerous underground caves and cave systems, which are both ecologically and historically significant.

Natural Resources:

Barbados' geography has shaped its natural resources, with the island being relatively limited in mineral wealth compared to some of its Caribbean neighbors. However, its fertile soils have historically supported a thriving agricultural sector, with sugar cane being a dominant crop during colonial times.

Today, the island's economy has diversified, and agriculture has shifted to focus on other crops such as vegetables, fruits, and flowers. Additionally, Barbados' coral reefs and marine ecosystems contribute to its burgeoning fishing and aquaculture industries.

Climate

This island gem, situated just outside the hurricane belt, offers visitors and residents an ideal environment for indulging in a variety of outdoor activities and immersing themselves in the beauty of its diverse landscapes.

Barbados experiences two primary seasons - the dry season and the wet season. The dry season typically spans from December to May, while the wet season extends from June to November.

Dry Season (December to May):

The dry season is considered the peak tourist season, attracting visitors seeking to escape colder climates and indulge in the island's warm embrace. During this period, the humidity is generally lower, and temperatures hover between 24°C to 31°C (75°F to 88°F). The skies are mostly clear, and rainfall is infrequent, making it an excellent time for beachgoers, water sports enthusiasts, and those who wish to explore the island's natural wonders.

Wet Season (June to November):

The wet season brings a refreshing change, with brief and intense bursts of tropical rain. The showers often pass quickly, allowing the sun to reemerge, creating lush and vibrant landscapes. Temperatures during the wet season remain relatively consistent, ranging from 25°C to 31°C (77°F to 88°F). Despite the occasional rainfall, this period also presents an opportunity for travelers to enjoy the island with fewer crowds, as it falls outside the peak tourist season.

Hurricane Season:

Barbados is fortunate to lie just beyond the typical hurricane belt, reducing the likelihood of direct hits by major hurricanes. However, like many Caribbean islands, Barbados is not immune to tropical storms or hurricanes during the official hurricane season, which runs from June to November. The island has comprehensive disaster preparedness plans in place to ensure the safety and well-being of residents and visitors alike.

Trade Winds:

The steady northeast trade winds that sweep across Barbados play a significant role in the island's climate. These gentle breezes provide natural air conditioning, moderating the temperatures and making the climate more comfortable. The trade winds are especially appreciated by visitors, as they provide relief from the warmth of the sun and create an ideal environment for sailing, windsurfing, and other water-based activities.

Microclimates:

Despite its small size, Barbados boasts diverse microclimates, each contributing to the island's unique charm. The eastern side of the island, exposed to the Atlantic Ocean, tends to be more rugged and receives slightly more rainfall than the sheltered western coast. The central highlands offer a cooler and lusher environment, providing fertile grounds for agriculture and tropical gardens.

Sunshine:

Barbados is renowned for its abundance of sunshine throughout the year. With an average of around 3,000 hours of sunshine annually, visitors can bask in the warm glow and soak up the Vitamin D. This sun-soaked climate contributes to the island's popularity as a top-notch destination for beach lovers and sun seekers.

Religion In Barbados

Religion in Barbados is an integral part of the island's cultural fabric, with a diverse array of beliefs and practices reflecting the nation's historical and cultural heritage. As a nation with a strong sense of community and tradition, religion plays a significant role in the daily lives of many Bajans (Barbadian people), influencing their values, celebrations, and social interactions.

Christianity:

Christianity is the predominant religion in Barbados, with the majority of the population identifying as Christian. The Anglican Church, a legacy of British colonial rule, has historically been the established church on the island. The Church of England's presence was significant, influencing the island's religious and cultural landscape for centuries.

In addition to Anglicanism, other Christian denominations have grown in prominence and popularity. The Roman Catholic Church has a considerable following, particularly among Bajans of Irish descent. Methodism, introduced to the island by Wesleyan missionaries, has also left a lasting impact on the religious landscape.

Other Christian denominations include Pentecostal, Baptist, and Seventh-day Adventist churches, which have gained considerable traction in recent years. These churches often offer vibrant worship experiences, fostering a sense of community and spiritual connection among their congregations.

Non-Christian Religions:

While Christianity is the dominant religion, Barbados also hosts a small but diverse community of people practicing non-Christian faiths. Islam has a presence on the island, with a mosque located in Bridgetown, and a growing number of Muslims contributing to the religious tapestry.

Hinduism is also practiced by a minority of the population, largely descended from Indian immigrants who arrived in the 19th and early 20th centuries to work on the sugar plantations. Hindu temples can be found in various areas of the island, serving as centers of worship and community gathering.

Religious Festivals and Celebrations:

Religious festivals and celebrations hold significant importance in Barbadian culture, with the entire community often coming together to participate in the festivities.

Easter, which commemorates the crucifixion and resurrection of Jesus Christ, is widely celebrated across the island. The Holy Week leading up to Easter Sunday sees churches holding processions, reenactments, and services to mark this sacred occasion.

Christmas is another major religious celebration, characterized by caroling, church services, and the exchange of gifts. The season also includes traditional culinary delights such as black cake and jug jug, which are enjoyed by families and friends.

Crop Over, originally a celebration of the sugar cane harvest, has evolved into a cultural festival that coincides with the end of the Christian season of Lent. While its origins are secular, many

Bajans view Crop Over as a time to celebrate and thank God for the year's successful harvest and blessings.

Social Impact and Values:

Religion in Barbados plays a significant role in shaping the social fabric of the society, instilling values of compassion, community, and a strong sense of moral responsibility. Religious institutions are often at the forefront of community development initiatives, providing support to vulnerable populations and contributing to charitable efforts.

Religious Spaces and Places of Worship:

Throughout the island, places of worship stand as symbols of faith and spirituality. Churches, temples, mosques, and synagogues can be found in various communities, serving as gathering points for worship, education, and social events.

Religious Tolerance:

Barbados is known for its religious tolerance, where people of different faiths coexist peacefully and respect each other's beliefs. This spirit of acceptance is deeply ingrained in the nation's culture, promoting an atmosphere of harmony and understanding among diverse religious communities.

Local Laws And Etiquette

As a nation with a rich cultural heritage, Bajans (Barbadian people) value their traditions and expect visitors to observe certain customs and behaviors. Additionally, adhering to the local laws is vital to maintaining a safe and harmonious environment for all.

Respect for Religion and Places of Worship: Barbados is a predominantly Christian country, and its residents hold their religious practices in high regard. Visitors should show respect when entering churches and other places of worship. Appropriate attire, such as covering shoulders and knees, is expected during religious services.

Appropriate Dress Code: While Barbados is a tropical destination known for its warm weather, modesty in attire is appreciated, especially when away from the beaches. When visiting public places, dining establishments, or shopping areas, avoid wearing swimwear or revealing clothing.

Respect for the Flag and Anthem: The Barbadian flag is a symbol of national pride and should be treated with respect. When the national anthem, "In Plenty and In Time of Need," is played at public events or gatherings, it is customary for everyone to stand in attention and show respect.

Polite and Courteous Behavior: Bajans are known for their warm hospitality, and polite behavior is highly valued. Simple gestures like saying "please" and "thank you," along with a friendly smile, go a long way in demonstrating respect and appreciation for the local culture.

Public Display of Affection: While public displays of affection are generally accepted, it is essential to exercise discretion and avoid excessive intimacy in public spaces, particularly in more conservative areas or religious sites.

Tipping and Service Charge: Tipping is not mandatory in Barbados, as a service charge is often included in the bill at restaurants and hotels. However, if you receive exceptional service, leaving a small tip as a token of appreciation is welcomed.

Drug Laws: Barbados has strict drug laws, and the possession, use, or trafficking of illegal substances can result in severe penalties, including imprisonment.

Beach Etiquette: Barbados is renowned for its beautiful beaches, and it is crucial to respect the natural environment and the privacy of others. Always follow local rules and regulations at public beaches, and avoid leaving trash behind.

Driving Laws: If you plan to rent a car and drive in Barbados, remember that vehicles drive on the left side of the road. Seatbelts are mandatory for both the driver and passengers. The legal drinking limit for driving is 35 micrograms of alcohol per 100 milliliters of breath.

Noise Regulations: Be mindful of noise levels, especially during late hours, as noise disturbances can be considered a breach of the peace and may lead to fines or penalties.

Photographing Locals: Always ask for permission before taking photos of local residents or their property, as it is a courteous gesture and a sign of respect for their privacy.

Preservation of Natural Resources: Barbados takes pride in its beautiful natural surroundings. Help maintain the island's pristine environment by avoiding littering, respecting wildlife, and refraining from damaging coral reefs while snorkeling or diving.

By embracing local laws and etiquette, visitors to Barbados can create positive and lasting impressions, forging connections with the warm-hearted Bajans and immersing themselves in the island's rich cultural heritage.

CHAPTER TWO

Health And Safety Tips For Visitors

The government of Barbados, along with various organizations and businesses, has made significant efforts to promote and enforce health and safety standards across the island.

Occupational Health and Safety: The Barbados government has enacted legislation to ensure that workplaces adhere to stringent health and safety regulations. The Barbados Occupational Safety and Health Act is in place to protect workers from potential hazards and ensure a safe working environment. Employers are required to provide appropriate safety training, protective gear, and equipment to their employees.

Food Safety: The Barbados Ministry of Health and Wellness closely monitors food establishments to maintain high standards of hygiene and safety. Food vendors and restaurants must adhere to strict guidelines to prevent foodborne illnesses and maintain a clean and safe environment for patrons.

Public Health Initiatives: The government has implemented various public health initiatives to combat the spread of communicable diseases. These initiatives include vaccination programs, health education campaigns, and regular health screenings to identify and manage health issues in the early stages.

Beach Safety: Barbados is renowned for its beautiful beaches, and the government takes beach safety seriously. Lifeguards are stationed at popular beaches to provide assistance and prevent accidents. Signs and flags indicate water conditions, and beachgoers are encouraged to follow safety guidelines to prevent drownings and water-related accidents.

Tourism Industry: Tourism is a significant contributor to Barbados' economy, and the government emphasizes the importance of ensuring the safety and well-being of tourists. Hotels, resorts, and tourist attractions must comply with safety standards to provide a secure and enjoyable experience for visitors.

Environmental Health: The government of Barbados actively promotes environmental health practices to safeguard the island's natural beauty and preserve its resources. Initiatives are in place to manage waste, promote recycling, and protect the environment from pollution.

Disaster Preparedness: Given its location in the hurricane-prone region, Barbados has a comprehensive disaster preparedness and response plan. This plan includes evacuation protocols, emergency shelters, and public awareness campaigns to prepare the population for potential natural disasters.

Healthcare Facilities: Barbados has a well-developed healthcare system with modern medical facilities and trained healthcare professionals. The government continually invests in improving healthcare services and infrastructure to ensure access to quality healthcare for all residents.

Road Safety: The government promotes road safety through public awareness campaigns and strict traffic regulations. This includes enforcing speed limits, seatbelt usage, and measures to prevent drunk driving to reduce road accidents and fatalities.

Money Matters And Currency Exchange

The official currency of Barbados is the Barbados Dollar (BBD), but the United States Dollar (USD) is also widely accepted. In fact, many businesses will give you change in BBD if you pay with USD.

If you're planning on visiting Barbados, you have a few options for exchanging your currency. You can:

Exchange your currency at a bank or currency exchange bureau.

Use a credit or debit card that doesn't charge foreign transaction fees.

Take out cash from an ATM.

Exchanging currency at a bank or currency exchange bureau

This is the most common way to exchange currency. You can find banks and currency exchange bureaus in most major cities and tourist destinations. The exchange rate you'll get will vary depending on the specific institution, so it's a good idea to shop around before you make a transaction.

Using a credit or debit card that doesn't charge foreign transaction fees

If you have a credit or debit card that doesn't charge foreign transaction fees, you can use it to make purchases in Barbados. This is a convenient option, as you won't have to worry about carrying around cash or exchanging your currency. However, it's important to note that your credit card company may still charge you a fee for using your card abroad.

Taking out cash from an ATM

You can also take out cash from an ATM in Barbados. This is a convenient option, as you can get cash whenever you need it. However, it's important to note that your bank may charge you a fee for using an ATM abroad. Additionally, the ATM itself may charge you a fee.

Which is the best way to use money in Barbados?

The best way to use money in Barbados depends on your individual preferences and circumstances. If you're comfortable carrying around cash, you can exchange your currency at a bank or currency exchange bureau. If you prefer to use your credit or debit card, you can find many businesses that accept them. And if you need cash in a hurry, you can take out money from an ATM.

Here are some additional tips for using money in Barbados:

Keep a small amount of cash on hand for small purchases and tips.

Be aware of the exchange rate when you're making purchases.

Ask about any fees that may be associated with using your credit or debit card abroad.

Keep track of your spending so you don't overspend.

Language In Barbados

The official language of Barbados is English, but the unique linguistic landscape of the island showcases a fascinating fusion of languages, dialects, and expressions that reflect the island's diverse heritage.

English: As the official language, English is widely used in government, education, media, and formal communication. Standard English is taught in schools, and it serves as the language of business and administration.

Bajan Creole: One of the most captivating aspects of language in Barbados is the Bajan Creole, also known as Bajan. This colorful and expressive Creole language has its roots in the West African languages brought by enslaved Africans during colonial times. Over the centuries, Bajan evolved with influences from English, West Indian languages, and elements of other African languages.

Bajan Creole is spoken informally among friends and family and serves as a symbol of cultural identity for Barbadians. It is infused with vivid local expressions, proverbs, and slang that add a unique charm to everyday conversations. For instance, "wuhloss" means "oh my goodness," "limin" means "hanging out," and "wuk-up" refers to a lively, rhythmic dance.

Language Evolution: Language in Barbados is a dynamic entity that constantly evolves and adapts. Younger generations might mix Bajan Creole with Standard English, creating what is commonly known as "Bajan English" or "Barbadian English." This linguistic fusion is an integral part of Barbados' cultural fabric, serving as a bridge between the island's historical roots and its modern identity.

Influence of Other Caribbean Languages: Due to its geographical location in the Caribbean, Barbados has been exposed to various regional languages and dialects. As a result, one can hear traces of other Caribbean languages, such as Jamaican Patois, Trinidadian Creole, and Vincentian Creole, influencing the local speech and expressions.

Language in Art and Music: The captivating language landscape of Barbados finds its way into the island's art and music. Local calypso and soca artists skillfully incorporate Bajan Creole into their lyrics, infusing their songs with a sense of cultural pride and authenticity. These musical expressions serve as a powerful means of preserving and celebrating the unique language of Barbados.

Multilingualism: Barbadians often display a high degree of multilingualism, switching effortlessly between languages depending on the context and the people they are interacting with. This ability to navigate between Standard English and Bajan Creole showcases the island's linguistic versatility and the deep-rooted connection that people have with their language.

Language in Barbados is a delightful mosaic that reflects the island's history, cultural diversity, and contemporary identity. With English as the official language and Bajan Creole as an essential part of everyday communication, Barbadians proudly embrace their linguistic heritage.

Communication And Internet Access

Communication and internet access in Barbados have undergone significant advancements in recent years, making it a well-connected and digitally empowered nation in the Caribbean region.

Telecommunication Infrastructure: Barbados has a robust telecommunication infrastructure that includes both landline and mobile networks. The country is well-covered by mobile services, and several telecom providers offer a range of communication packages to residents and visitors. Mobile phones are widely used for communication, both for voice calls and internet access.

Internet Connectivity: Barbados boasts a reliable and high-speed internet connection. The country has invested in developing its broadband infrastructure, resulting in widespread access to fast and stable internet services. Residents and businesses enjoy a range of options from various internet service providers (ISPs) that offer fiber optic and cable internet services.

Digital Transformation: Barbados has been actively embracing the digital era, with a focus on digital transformation in various sectors. E-government initiatives have made public services more accessible online, facilitating easier communication between citizens and government agencies.

Internet Penetration: Internet penetration in Barbados is relatively high, with a significant percentage of the population having access to the internet. This level of connectivity has enabled the widespread use of digital technologies in various aspects of daily life, such as education, business, healthcare, and entertainment.

Public Wi-Fi: Many public spaces in Barbados, including airports, libraries, and certain tourist areas, offer free public Wi-Fi access. This initiative promotes connectivity for residents and tourists, allowing them to stay connected while on the move.

Telecommunications Regulation: The telecommunications sector in Barbados is regulated by the Fair Trading Commission, which ensures fair competition among telecom providers and monitors service quality and pricing to protect consumers' interests.

Internet Service Providers: Several ISPs operate in Barbados, providing a competitive market for internet services. Popular ISPs include Digicel, Flow, and TeleBarbados, among others. They offer a range of plans to cater to different needs, from residential to business users.

Social Media and Communication Apps: Social media platforms and communication apps are widely used in Barbados for staying connected with friends and family. Platforms like WhatsApp, Facebook, Instagram, and Twitter are immensely popular for sharing updates and communicating with others.

Digital Inclusion: The government of Barbados recognizes the importance of digital inclusion and aims to bridge the digital divide. Efforts are made to ensure that all citizens have access to the internet and digital technologies, even in rural and remote areas.

Cybersecurity: As digital technologies become more integrated into daily life, cybersecurity has become a significant concern. The government of Barbados is taking steps to strengthen cybersecurity measures and protect individuals and businesses from online threats.

Packing Essential List For Visitors

The island's tropical climate and diverse attractions require a well-thought-out packing list. Here is a list of packing essentials for visitors traveling to Barbados:

Clothing:

Lightweight and breathable clothing: Pack light, airy fabrics like cotton or linen to stay comfortable in the tropical heat.

Swimwear: With stunning beaches all around, you'll definitely want to take a dip in the Caribbean Sea.

Beach cover-ups: Useful for heading to and from the beach or pool.

Sun hat and sunglasses: Protect yourself from the strong sun rays.

Light rain jacket or umbrella: Tropical showers are common, especially during the rainy season.

Casual wear: Comfortable clothes for exploring the island and enjoying its attractions.

Dressy outfits: Some upscale restaurants or events may require slightly more formal attire.

Footwear:

Sandals/flip-flops: Perfect for the beach and warm weather.

Comfortable walking shoes: You'll likely be exploring various attractions, so comfortable footwear is essential.

Dress shoes: For more formal outings or dinners.

Travel Documents:

Passport and visa (if required): Ensure your passport is valid for at least six months beyond your travel dates.

Flight tickets and itinerary: Keep all travel-related documents organized.

Travel insurance: Consider purchasing travel insurance that covers medical emergencies and trip cancellations.

Sun Protection:

Sunscreen: High SPF sunscreen to protect your skin from the strong sun.

Aloe vera gel or after-sun lotion: In case of sunburn.

Personal Care:

Toiletries: Bring your preferred personal care items, including shampoo, conditioner, soap, and any specific skincare products you may need.

Insect repellent: To protect against mosquitoes, especially in the evenings.

Medications: Bring any prescription medications and a basic first-aid kit.

Electronics:

Camera: Capture the beauty of Barbados.

Mobile phone and charger: Stay connected and navigate using map apps.

Universal adapter: Barbados uses Type A and Type B power outlets.

Beach Gear:

Beach towel: Some accommodations may not provide beach towels.

Snorkeling gear: Bring your own snorkel and mask or consider renting on the island.

Beach bag: Carry your essentials to the beach.

Miscellaneous:

Reusable water bottle: Stay hydrated while exploring the island.

Cash and credit cards: While credit cards are widely accepted, it's good to have some cash on hand for smaller transactions.

Travel guide or maps: Help you navigate and learn about the island's attractions.

Optional:

Daypack or small backpack: Ideal for day trips and excursions.

Portable umbrella or beach tent: Provide additional shade on the beach.

Remember to pack light and efficiently, leaving room for souvenirs and other items you might want to bring back home.

CHAPTER THREE
The Perfect Season To Visit Barbados

Barbados enjoys a warm and sunny climate year-round, but there are distinct seasons that may suit different travelers. Here's a breakdown of the seasons to help you decide the best time to visit:

High Season (December to April):

Weather: This is the dry season, characterized by warm temperatures, low humidity, and minimal rainfall. It's an excellent time to escape colder climates and bask in the sunshine.

Events: The high season coincides with several festivals and events, including the Barbados Food and Rum Festival, Holetown Festival, and various regattas. The island is abuzz with cultural and sporting activities.

Crowd Levels: The high season attracts a significant number of tourists, especially during Christmas, New Year, and the Easter holidays. Accommodation and flights may be pricier, and popular attractions can get crowded.

Shoulder Season (May to June and November):

Weather: The shoulder season marks the transition between the dry and rainy seasons. Temperatures remain warm, and there might be occasional short showers, but overall, it's a pleasant time to visit.

Events: While there might be fewer events compared to the high season, you can still find some local festivals and activities during this time.

Crowd Levels: The crowds are generally thinner compared to the high season, making it a good time to visit if you prefer a more relaxed and laid-back atmosphere.

Low Season (July to October):

Weather: The low season is the rainy season in Barbados, with higher chances of tropical showers and occasional thunderstorms. However, the rain usually comes in short bursts, and the island remains lush and green.

Events: The low season is relatively quieter in terms of events and festivals. Some businesses and attractions may close for renovations during this time.

Crowd Levels: This is the least crowded time to visit Barbados. You'll have more space on the beaches and better opportunities to interact with the locals.

Ultimately, the perfect season to visit Barbados depends on your personal preferences. If you prefer warm, dry weather and a vibrant atmosphere with plenty of events, the high season from December to April might be ideal. On the other hand, if you're seeking a more relaxed and budget-friendly experience with fewer crowds, consider visiting during the shoulder or low seasons.

How To Get There

As a popular tourist destination, Barbados is well-connected to various parts of the world. There are several ways for visitors to get to Barbados:

By Air:

Grantley Adams International Airport (BGI): This is the only international airport in Barbados, located in Christ Church Parish. It serves as the main gateway for visitors traveling to the island by air. Many major airlines offer direct flights to Barbados from various cities in North America, Europe, and other parts of the Caribbean.

Connecting Flights: If there are no direct flights from your location, you can opt for connecting flights through major hubs in the United States, Canada, Europe, or other Caribbean islands.

By Cruise:

Cruise Ship Arrivals: Barbados is a popular port of call for many cruise lines, and you can visit the island on a Caribbean cruise itinerary. Cruise ships dock at the Bridgetown Cruise Terminal, where visitors can disembark and explore the island.

By Private Yacht:

For those with their own yachts, Barbados is a fantastic destination to sail to. The island has several marinas and anchorages for private yacht travelers.

Travel Protocols:

Due to the COVID-19 pandemic, there might be specific travel protocols and requirements in place for visitors. This may include pre-arrival testing, vaccination, health forms, or quarantine measures. It's essential to check the latest travel advisories and requirements before planning your trip.

Transportation on the Island:

Once you arrive in Barbados, there are various transportation options available. Taxis and rental cars are readily available at the airport. Additionally, many hotels and resorts offer airport transfers for their guests. Public buses and private minivans (known as "ZRs") provide affordable transportation throughout the island.

Visa And Entry Requirements

Visa requirements

Citizens of most countries do not need a visa to visit Barbados for stays of up to 6 months. However, it is always a good idea to check with the Barbados Immigration Department to confirm the visa requirements for your nationality.

Citizens of certain countries, such as China, India, and Russia, do need a visa to visit Barbados. These visas can be obtained from the Barbados High Commission or Embassy in your home country.

If you are unsure whether you need a visa to visit Barbados, you can check the Barbados Immigration Department website.

Entry requirements

In addition to a valid passport, all visitors to Barbados must meet the following entry requirements:

A completed Barbados ED Immigration Card. This card can be obtained from the airline you are flying with or from the Barbados Immigration Department website.

A valid return ticket or proof of onward travel.

Sufficient funds to cover your stay.

Health insurance that covers medical costs in Barbados.

Proof of accommodation.

Children traveling to Barbados

Children under the age of 18 who are traveling to Barbados without their parents must have a letter of authorization from their parents. This letter must be signed by both parents and must include the following information:

The names and contact information of the parents and child.

The dates of the child's travel.

The purpose of the child's travel.

The name and contact information of the person who will be accompanying the child in Barbados.

Pets traveling to Barbados

Pets are allowed to enter Barbados, but they must meet certain requirements. Pets must be accompanied by a valid health certificate from a veterinarian and must be quarantined for 10 days upon arrival.

Getting Around On Arrival

Whether you prefer exploring on your own or relying on local services, there are several options available to suit your preferences and budget. Here's a glimpse on how visitors can get around Barbados:

Public Transportation: Barbados has a reliable and affordable public transportation system, primarily consisting of buses. The bright blue government-operated buses are a common sight on the island and offer an extensive network of routes covering most major towns and attractions. The bus fare is reasonable, making it an economical option for travelers. You can catch a bus at designated bus stops or simply flag one down along the main roads.

ZR Vans and Mini-Buses: In addition to the government buses, visitors can also use privately-owned mini-buses and vans, locally known as "ZR vans." These smaller vehicles follow specific routes and are easily recognizable by their distinctive yellow license plates. ZR vans are known for playing loud music and offering a more lively and adventurous ride. While they can be crowded, they provide an authentic Barbadian experience and are an excellent way to interact with locals.

Taxis: Taxis are readily available in Barbados and offer a more private and personalized mode of transportation. Taxis operate both on fixed rates and metered fares, depending on the type of taxi service you choose. Official taxis are marked with "Z" on their license plates and are regulated by the government. It's always a good idea to confirm the fare with the driver before starting your journey.

Renting a Car: For those seeking greater independence and flexibility in their explorations, renting a car is a popular option. Several international car rental companies have branches in Barbados, and local agencies also offer rental services. Keep in mind that Barbados follows left-hand driving, and you'll need to obtain a temporary driving permit from your rental agency or the Barbados Licensing Authority.

Scooters and Mopeds: If you're comfortable riding a scooter or moped, it can be an enjoyable and efficient way to navigate the island's narrow roads and beat traffic. Rentals are available, but make sure you have the necessary permits and safety gear.

Walking: Exploring Barbados on foot can be a rewarding experience, especially in areas like Bridgetown and along the west coast. Many attractions, shops, restaurants, and beaches are within walking distance in these areas. Just remember to stay hydrated, wear comfortable footwear, and be mindful of the tropical heat.

Private Tours and Excursions: For a more curated and guided experience, consider booking private tours and excursions. Many tour operators offer a range of options, from island sightseeing tours to snorkeling adventures and catamaran cruises.

Overall, getting around Barbados as a visitor is straightforward and allows you to experience the island's beauty, culture, and warm hospitality.

Public Transportation

When visiting the beautiful island nation of Barbados, exploring its vibrant culture, stunning beaches, and historical sites is made easier by the well-developed and efficient public transportation system. Whether you're a budget-conscious traveler or simply want to experience the local way of getting around, Barbados offers several convenient options for public transportation.

1. Buses:

Barbados boasts an extensive network of colorful and easily recognizable government-owned buses. These buses are a popular choice for both locals and visitors due to their affordability and coverage of most major tourist destinations. The primary bus terminal, called the "Fairchild Street Terminal," is located in Bridgetown, the capital city. From here, buses radiate outwards to various parts of the island.

Buses are divided into two types: blue buses and yellow buses. The blue buses are larger, air-conditioned, and cater more towards longer routes, while the yellow buses are smaller and serve shorter distances. Both types are safe and comfortable.

2. ZR Vans:

One unique mode of transportation in Barbados is the privately-owned "ZR" vans. These are minivans that are often colorfully decorated and play loud music. While they might not be as formal as the government buses, they are an adventurous and authentic way to experience local culture. ZR vans have set routes and can be hailed from the side of the road. They are known for their fast pace and occasional stops for passengers along the way.

3. Taxis:

Taxis in Barbados are readily available and can be found at tourist areas, hotels, and near the airport. While taxis offer the convenience of personalized transportation, they are generally more expensive compared to buses and ZR vans. It's advisable to negotiate the fare before starting the journey or ensure the meter is used.

4. Renting a Car:

For those who want the utmost flexibility in exploring the island, renting a car is a viable option. Barbados has a well-maintained road network with clear signage. However, it's important to note that driving is on the left side of the road, as the country follows British driving rules.

5. Public Transportation Etiquette:

When using public transportation in Barbados, there are a few etiquette points to keep in mind:

Fares: Buses and ZR vans often require exact change in local currency (Barbadian dollars). It's a good idea to carry small bills and coins.

Courtesy: Locals are generally friendly and helpful, so don't hesitate to ask for assistance or directions.

Timeliness: While the public transportation system is reliable, schedules might not be as rigid as in some other countries. Be prepared for a slight variation in arrival and departure times.

6. Payment Options:

Cash is the most widely accepted form of payment for public transportation. If you plan to use public transportation extensively, consider purchasing a prepaid transportation card from the Barbados Transport Board, which can save you money and time.

Car Rental

When planning a visit to the idyllic Caribbean island of Barbados, one prudent choice for optimizing your travel experience is availing yourself of car rental services. The picturesque landscapes, cultural diversity, and numerous attractions of the island become even more accessible and enjoyable when navigating them at your own pace. This guide provides visitors with valuable insights into the intricacies of car rental services in Barbados, ensuring a seamless and enriching exploration of this tropical paradise.

1. Selection of Rental Company: Barbados offers a plethora of rental companies catering to the discerning traveler. It is advisable to conduct thorough research prior to your trip, evaluating factors such as reputation, customer reviews, and the extent of their service network. A well-established company with a reputation for exceptional customer service and transparent practices is an ideal choice.

2. Preemptive Reservations: To ensure availability, secure competitive rates, and mitigate any last-minute challenges, advance reservations are highly recommended, especially during peak tourist seasons. Early booking not only guarantees access to a preferred vehicle but also contributes to a stress-free vacation planning process.

3. Licensing and Age Prerequisites: To facilitate the car rental process, visitors must possess a valid driver's license from their country of residence. While requirements may vary among rental providers, the minimum age for renting a car generally falls within the range of 21 to 25 years. Some rental companies might stipulate supplementary fees for drivers below a certain age threshold.

4. Adherence to Driving Regulations: Barbados adheres to the left-hand driving convention, aligned with British driving regulations. Acquainting oneself with this distinctive driving orientation before embarking on journeys is crucial for safety and overall road compliance.

5. Comprehensive Insurance Options: Rental companies typically offer diverse insurance plans, ranging from basic coverage to enhanced options for comprehensive protection. It is advisable to engage in a detailed discussion with the rental agency representative to comprehend the scope of coverage, including potential deductibles and limitations.

6. Diverse Vehicle Selection: A diverse fleet of vehicles catering to varying preferences and group sizes awaits visitors in Barbados. Options span from compact cars to SUVs and even luxury vehicles. Selecting a vehicle suited to your itinerary and travel companions is pivotal for a comfortable and enjoyable exploration of the island.

7. Navigation Solutions: While Barbados is relatively compact, having a GPS navigation system at one's disposal can significantly enhance the navigational experience. Many rental companies provide GPS rentals or incorporate them as supplementary services, thereby facilitating efficient exploration even in less-frequented locales.

8. Road Conditions and Traffic Considerations: The main thoroughfares of Barbados exhibit satisfactory maintenance standards, although rural roads may vary in infrastructure. Urban areas might experience traffic congestion during peak hours, warranting prudent route planning to optimize travel time.

9. Parking Facilities: Parking facilities are commonly available at tourist attractions, beaches, and dining establishments across the island. Familiarize yourself with local parking regulations, as some locations may entail fees for usage.

10. Exploring the Island: The liberty afforded by a rental car in Barbados unveils the possibility of personalized exploration, encompassing the vibrant capital of Bridgetown, the serene Bathsheba beaches, and the historical allure of plantation estates. This self-directed journey ensures an immersive encounter with the island's natural beauty and cultural splendor.

11. Fuel Accessibility: Fuel stations are conveniently dispersed throughout Barbados. These stations usually offer full-service fueling, and payment options encompass both cash and credit cards.

12. Local Etiquette and Safety: Adhering to local driving norms, exercising caution, and abiding by speed limits (typically ranging from 40 to 60 km/h) contribute to road safety. Additionally, compliance with mandatory seat belt usage for all passengers is a fundamental safety requirement

Car rental services in Barbados offer visitors an opportunity to transcend the conventional tourist experience and engage in an intimate exploration of the island's myriad wonders.

Accommodation Options

When visiting Barbados, visitors have a range of accommodation options to choose from, including hotels, resorts, villas, and guesthouses.

Hotels and resorts in Barbados offer a range of amenities and services, including restaurants, bars, swimming pools, and spa facilities. Some of the popular hotels and resorts in Barbados include The Crane Resort, Sandals Barbados, and Fairmont Royal Pavilion.

Villas are another popular accommodation option in Barbados, particularly for visitors who are traveling with family or a group. Villas offer privacy and space and often come equipped with a kitchen, living room, and outdoor areas such as a private pool or patio. Some of the popular villa rental companies in Barbados include Blue Sky Luxury and Barbados Villas.

Guesthouses and bed and breakfasts are also available in Barbados and offer a more local and authentic experience. Guesthouses are often smaller and more intimate than hotels and resorts and are located in residential neighborhoods or near popular attractions. Some of the popular guesthouses in Barbados include Peach and Quiet and Sea-U Guest House.

Overall, visitors to Barbados have a range of accommodation options to choose from, depending on their budget, travel preferences, and desired level of luxury and amenities.

Luxury Hotels And Resorts

Barbados is a stunning Caribbean island that offers visitors a range of luxury hotels and resorts to choose from. With its beautiful beaches, vibrant culture, and warm climate, Barbados is a popular destination for travelers seeking a luxurious and indulgent vacation experience. Let's take a look at some of the top luxury hotels and resorts in Barbados, along with their prices and amenities.

Sandy Lane

Sandy Lane is one of the most exclusive luxury resorts in Barbados, known for its world-class amenities and stunning location on the island's west coast. The resort boasts 112 luxurious rooms and suites, each featuring elegant decor, marble bathrooms, and private balconies or terraces with views of the Caribbean Sea or the resort's lush gardens. The resort offers a range of amenities, including three golf courses, a state-of-the-art fitness center, a full-service spa, and nine tennis courts.

Price: Room rates at Sandy Lane start at $1,000 per night and can go up to $25,000 per night for the resort's five-bedroom villa.

The Crane Resort

The Crane Resort is a luxurious beachfront resort located on the southeastern coast of Barbados. The resort features a range of accommodation options, including one, two, and three-bedroom suites and private villas with their own plunge pools. The resort's amenities include five outdoor pools, a full-service spa, and several restaurants and bars.

Price: Room rates at The Crane Resort start at $500 per night for a one-bedroom suite and can go up to $1,500 per night for a three-bedroom penthouse.

Cobblers Cove

Cobblers Cove is a luxurious boutique hotel located on the island's west coast. The hotel features 40 spacious suites, each featuring elegant decor, luxurious linens, and views of the Caribbean Sea or the hotel's tropical gardens. The hotel's amenities include a full-service spa, a freshwater pool, and a restaurant serving international and Caribbean cuisine.

Price: Room rates at Cobblers Cove start at $600 per night for a garden suite and can go up to $1,400 per night for a two-bedroom suite.

Fairmont Royal Pavilion

The Fairmont Royal Pavilion is a luxurious beachfront resort located on the west coast of Barbados. The resort features 72 luxurious rooms and suites, each featuring elegant decor, private balconies or patios, and stunning views of the Caribbean Sea. The resort's amenities include a full-service spa, a freshwater pool, and several restaurants and bars.

Price: Room rates at the Fairmont Royal Pavilion start at $600 per night for a deluxe oceanfront room and can go up to $1,800 per night for a three-bedroom villa.

Coral Reef Club

Coral Reef Club is a luxurious boutique hotel located on the west coast of Barbados. The hotel features 88 elegant rooms and suites, each featuring a private patio or balcony with views of the hotel's lush gardens. The hotel's amenities include a full-service spa, two freshwater pools, and a restaurant serving international and Caribbean cuisine.

Price: Room rates at Coral Reef Club start at $450 per night for a garden room and can go up to $1,000 per night for a luxury cottage suite.

The Sandpiper

The Sandpiper is a luxurious boutique hotel located on the west coast of Barbados. The hotel features 48 elegantly designed rooms and suites, each featuring a private patio or balcony with views of the hotel's lush gardens. The hotel's amenities include a full-service spa, a freshwater pool, and a restaurant serving international and Caribbean cuisine.

Price: Room rates at The Sandpiper start at $475 per night for a garden room and can go up to $1,200 per night for a one-bedroom suite with a private pool.

Saint Peter's Bay

Saint Peter's Bay is a luxurious beachfront resort located on the north-west coast of Barbados. The resort features 57 spacious three-bedroom apartments, each featuring elegant decor, modern amenities, and stunning views of the Caribbean Sea. The resort's amenities include a full-service spa, a freshwater pool, and a beachfront restaurant and bar.

Price: Room rates at Saint Peter's Bay start at $1,200 per night for a three-bedroom apartment.

The House by Elegant Hotels

The House by Elegant Hotels is a luxurious adult-only beachfront hotel located on the west coast of Barbados. The hotel features 34 elegantly designed rooms and suites, each featuring a private patio or balcony with views of the Caribbean Sea. The hotel's amenities include a full-service spa, a freshwater pool, and a restaurant serving international and Caribbean cuisine.

Price: Room rates at The House by Elegant Hotels start at $500 per night for a junior suite and can go up to $1,000 per night for a one-bedroom suite with a private pool.

Waves Hotel and Spa

Waves Hotel and Spa is a luxurious beachfront resort located on the west coast of Barbados. The resort features 70 modern rooms and suites, each featuring elegant decor, modern amenities, and views of the Caribbean Sea or the hotel's lush gardens. The resort's amenities include a full-service spa, three freshwater pools, and several restaurants and bars.

Price: Room rates at Waves Hotel and Spa start at $400 per night for a standard guest room and can go up to $1,000 per night for a penthouse suite.

The Sandals Royal Barbados

The Sandals Royal Barbados is an all-inclusive beachfront resort located on the south coast of Barbados. The resort features 222 luxurious rooms and suites, each featuring elegant decor, modern amenities, and views of the Caribbean Sea or the resort's lush gardens. The resort's amenities include 11 restaurants, seven bars, a full-service spa, and several outdoor pools.

Price: Room rates at The Sandals Royal Barbados start at $800 per night for a deluxe room and can go up to $4,000 per night for a presidential suite.

Barbados offers visitors a range of luxurious hotels and resorts, each featuring elegant decor, modern amenities, and stunning views of the Caribbean Sea. Prices for these accommodations can vary depending on the location, amenities, and time of year. However, visitors can expect to pay anywhere from $400 to $25,000 per night for a luxurious stay in Barbados.

Boutique Hotels And Guesthouses

Boutique hotels and guesthouses in Barbados are typically located in historic buildings or renovated properties that have been transformed into stylish and modern accommodations. Many boutique properties feature unique and eclectic decor, showcasing local art and design elements that reflect the island's vibrant culture and heritage.

One of the benefits of staying at a boutique hotel or guesthouse in Barbados is the personalized attention and service that guests receive. The smaller size of these properties allows staff to offer a more tailored and attentive experience, with a focus on guest satisfaction and comfort.

Boutique hotels and guesthouses in Barbados offer a range of amenities and services, including on-site dining options, swimming pools, spa facilities, and personalized concierge services. Some properties may also offer beach access, water sports rentals, and other recreational activities.

One of the most popular boutique properties in Barbados is The Atlantis Hotel, located on the island's east coast in the historic fishing village of Tent Bay. The Atlantis Hotel features 10 guest rooms and suites, each individually decorated with antique furnishings and original artwork. The property also features a restaurant that specializes in farm-to-table cuisine, with ingredients sourced from local farmers and fishermen.

Another popular boutique property in Barbados is Little Arches Boutique Hotel, located in the charming seaside town of Oistins. This adults-only hotel features 10 rooms and suites, each designed with a blend of modern and traditional Caribbean style. The property also features an on-site restaurant, a rooftop terrace with a plunge pool, and personalized concierge services.

Guesthouses are another popular choice for visitors to Barbados who are looking for a more local and authentic experience. Guesthouses are typically smaller and more intimate than hotels and offer a range of room options, from private rooms with shared bathrooms to larger suites with en-suite facilities.

Guesthouses in Barbados are often located in residential neighborhoods or in close proximity to popular attractions and beaches. Many guesthouses offer personalized concierge services, along with on-site dining options and recreational activities such as yoga classes or water sports rentals.

One of the most popular guesthouses in Barbados is Peach and Quiet, located on the island's south coast in the town of Inch Marlow. This beachfront property features eight guest rooms and suites, each designed with a blend of traditional Caribbean style and modern amenities. The property also features an on-site restaurant, a swimming pool, and personalized concierge services.

Sea-U Guest House is another popular guesthouse in Barbados, located on the island's east coast in the historic town of Bathsheba. This property features 10 guest rooms and suites, each designed with a unique and eclectic decor that reflects the island's natural beauty and local culture. The property also features an on-site restaurant, a yoga pavilion, and personalized concierge services.

When choosing a boutique hotel or guesthouse in Barbados, visitors should consider their budget, travel preferences, and desired level of luxury and amenities. Many boutique properties in Barbados offer packages and specials throughout the year, making it easier for visitors to find the perfect accommodation option that fits their needs and budget.

Camping And Eco-Tourism

Barbados, the easternmost island in the Caribbean, offers a diverse range of accommodation options for visitors seeking eco-friendly and sustainable tourism experiences. Camping and eco-tourism accommodations are popular among adventurous travelers looking to immerse themselves in the island's natural beauty and unique culture.

Camping is an affordable and enjoyable way to experience the outdoors while staying close to nature. There are several camping sites in Barbados, ranging from beachfront locations to inland forests. One of the most popular camping sites is the Lion's Den in St. Joseph. This site is located in the heart of the island's lush countryside and offers stunning views of the East Coast. The campsite provides amenities such as showers, toilets, and outdoor cooking facilities. It also has a communal area where campers can relax and socialize with other travelers.

Another popular camping site is the Bathsheba Surf Village in St. Joseph. This site is located near the famous Bathsheba beach, known for its rugged beauty and excellent surfing conditions. The campsite offers a unique camping experience in a tropical forest setting, complete with communal fire pits, hammocks, and outdoor showers. Visitors can choose to rent a tent or bring their own equipment. The site also has a small kitchen area where campers can prepare their meals.

For those who prefer a more luxurious camping experience, the Eco Lifestyle Lodge in St. George offers a glamping option. The lodge's tents are furnished with comfortable beds, fans, and solar-powered lighting. The tents are set in a serene forested area, surrounded by tropical flora and fauna. The lodge also has a restaurant that serves delicious local cuisine made with organic ingredients.

In addition to camping, Barbados offers several eco-tourism accommodation options that promote sustainable tourism practices. These accommodations include eco-resorts, guesthouses, and villas that are designed to minimize their environmental impact while providing guests with a unique and comfortable experience.

One of the most popular eco-resorts in Barbados is the Atlantis Hotel in St. Joseph. This historic hotel was built in the 1800s and has been renovated to incorporate sustainable features such as rainwater harvesting and solar power. The hotel's rooms are designed to capture the island's natural beauty, with many offering stunning views of the ocean or the countryside. The hotel also has an organic garden and a restaurant that serves locally sourced and seasonal cuisine.

Another eco-resort that is worth considering is the Little Arches Boutique Hotel in Christ Church. This hotel has a strong focus on sustainability, with features such as solar power, rainwater harvesting, and composting. The hotel's rooms are decorated with a mix of contemporary and traditional Caribbean design elements, creating a unique and stylish atmosphere. The hotel also has an onsite restaurant that serves healthy and locally sourced meals.

For those who prefer a more intimate and authentic experience, guesthouses and villas are great options. These accommodations are often run by local families who are passionate about showcasing their culture and promoting sustainable tourism practices.

The Sugar Bay Barbados Resort in Christ Church is an excellent example of an eco-friendly villa. This resort is set on a 5-acre property that features lush gardens and a private beach. The resort's villas are designed to blend in with the natural surroundings and are equipped with sustainable features such as rainwater harvesting and solar power. The villas also have private plunge pools and outdoor showers, creating a luxurious and relaxing atmosphere.

Another great option for eco-tourism accommodation in Barbados is the Inchcape Seaside Villas in Christ Church. These villas are located on the island's southern coast, overlooking the Atlantic Ocean. The villas are built using sustainable materials and are designed to provide guests with a comfortable and authentic Caribbean experience. Each villa has its own private terrace, outdoor shower, and direct access to the beach.

In addition to providing eco-friendly accommodations, many of these establishments offer activities and tours that allow visitors to connect with nature and learn about the island's unique culture and history.

For example, the Atlantis Hotel offers guided tours of the nearby coastline, where visitors can learn about the island's geology, flora, and fauna. The Little Arches Boutique Hotel offers yoga classes and paddleboarding tours, which allow guests to explore the island's beautiful coastline in a sustainable and low-impact way.

The Sugar Bay Barbados Resort offers a range of activities that promote sustainability and environmental conservation, such as beach cleanups and turtle monitoring programs. The resort also has an onsite marine education center, where visitors can learn about the island's marine ecosystems and the importance of conservation.

Inchcape Seaside Villas offer guests the opportunity to experience the island's vibrant culture and history through tours and workshops. Visitors can learn about the island's rich history of rum production, take a cooking class to learn about traditional Bajan cuisine, or visit local artisans to learn about traditional crafts such as pottery and basket weaving.

Overall, Barbados offers a wealth of eco-tourism accommodations and activities for visitors who are passionate about sustainability and environmental conservation. Whether you choose to camp in the island's beautiful forests or stay in an eco-resort that prioritizes sustainable practices, you are sure to have a unique and memorable experience that connects you with nature and the local community.

CHAPTER FOUR

Food And Drink In Barbados

Welcome to the culinary tapestry of Barbados, a sun-kissed jewel nestled in the embrace of the Caribbean Sea. As you embark on a gastronomic adventure across this enchanting island, prepare to be captivated by the vibrant flavors, tantalizing aromas, and warm hospitality that define Barbadian cuisine.

Picture yourself strolling along the golden shores, where the salty breeze carries whispers of sizzling seafood and fragrant spices from the open-air grills of beachside shacks. The heart of Barbadian cuisine beats to the rhythm of the sea, and its seafood offerings are a testament to this relationship. Indulge in succulent flying fish, the island's national dish, prepared with a delicate blend of herbs and spices that evoke the essence of the Caribbean. The fish, tender and flaky, is often paired with cou-cou, a unique dish made from cornmeal and okra, forming a harmonious marriage of textures and flavors that will linger in your memory.

For those seeking a fusion of tradition and innovation, the island's bustling capital, Bridgetown, beckons with its array of eateries. Discover the fiery heat of Bajan pepper sauce, a condiment that packs a punch and infuses a burst of zesty excitement into every dish. As you explore the streets, tantalizing aromas lead you to stalls offering freshly fried fish cakes, known locally as "cutters," nestled in salt bread and garnished with a medley of pickled vegetables. The amalgamation of tastes and textures reflects the island's rich history, a tapestry woven with influences from Africa, India, and Europe.

Venturing further inland, lush plantations paint a verdant backdrop for culinary escapades. Sample the famed Barbadian pudding and souse, a harmonious juxtaposition of sweet and savory. Pudding, a mixture of sweet potato, grated coconut, and spices, is slow-cooked until it forms a rich, caramelized crust. Souse, on the other hand, offers a savory contrast with pickled pork or chicken, marinated in a zesty mixture of lime, cucumber, and onion.

As the sun dips below the horizon, the island transforms into a paradise for nocturnal explorations. Embrace the rhythms of reggae and soca music as they envelop you in a symphony of Caribbean spirit. The atmospheric beach bars and rum shops come alive, offering an array of potent concoctions crafted from Barbados' most cherished export – rum. Sip on the world-renowned Mount Gay Rum, aged to perfection, or sample cocktails infused with tropical fruits like coconut, mango, and pineapple.

No culinary journey through Barbados is complete without experiencing its delectable desserts. Treat your taste buds to the delightful sweetness of coconut bread, a moist and tender loaf with shreds of coconut woven throughout. For the ultimate indulgence, relish the velvety embrace of sweet potato pie, crowned with a dollop of freshly whipped cream.

Local Cuisine And Specialties To Try Out

From beachside shacks to upscale restaurants, here are some local cuisine and specialties you must try during your visit:

1. Flying Fish and Cou-Cou: Indulge in Barbados' national dish, a marriage of flavors that symbolizes the island's affinity with the sea. Delicate flying fish, seasoned with local herbs and spices, are paired with cou-cou, a unique dish made from cornmeal and okra. The fish's tender texture contrasts beautifully with the creamy cou-cou, creating a dish that's both comforting and captivating.

2. Pudding and Souse: A quintessential Bajan delight, pudding and souse is a blend of sweet and savory. Pudding, a sweet potato-based dish with grated coconut and spices, is slow-cooked to perfection. Souse features pickled pork or chicken marinated in a tangy mixture of lime, cucumber, and onion. The harmonious pairing of these two contrasting elements is a true taste of Barbadian culture.

3. Bajan Pepper Sauce: For those who relish a touch of heat, Bajan pepper sauce is a must-try condiment. Made from fiery Scotch bonnet peppers, onions, and other spices, this sauce adds a kick to any dish. Be cautious—it's not for the faint of heart, but it will surely awaken your taste buds.

4. Cutters: When you're craving a quick, flavorful bite, seek out cutters—Bajan-style sandwiches made with salt bread. These delicious handheld treats are usually filled with fish, ham, cheese, or egg, along with a medley of pickled vegetables. They're perfect for a satisfying meal on the go.

5. Macaroni Pie: A comfort food staple, macaroni pie is a creamy, cheesy casserole that has its roots in British influence. This Bajan twist on mac and cheese features macaroni pasta baked with a blend of eggs, milk, and local spices. It's a beloved side dish that complements various main courses.

6. Conkies: If you're visiting around Independence Day (November 30th), be sure to try conkies. These sweet treats are made from cornmeal, grated pumpkin, coconut, raisins, and spices, all wrapped in banana leaves and steamed. Conkies celebrate Barbados' culture and history and are a delightfully unique experience.

7. Fish Cakes: Fish cakes are a popular street food that blends the island's love for seafood and spices. These savory bites feature a mixture of salted cod, flour, herbs, and seasonings, deep-fried to golden perfection. They're often enjoyed as a snack or appetizer.

8. Rum Delights: Barbados is renowned for its rum, so be sure to savor this island spirit in various forms. Try rum punches, cocktails, or even enjoy a rum tasting at one of the local distilleries. And don't forget to explore the many rum-infused desserts, such as rum cake and rum ice cream.

9. Coconut Bread: Satisfy your sweet tooth with a slice of coconut bread. This delightful treat features tender shreds of coconut woven into a moist, slightly sweet bread. Enjoy it as a breakfast option or an afternoon snack.

10. Fresh Tropical Fruits: While not unique to Barbados, the island's tropical fruits are a refreshing delight. Enjoy the succulent sweetness of mangoes, pineapples, guavas, and passion fruits. These flavors are a testament to the lushness of the Caribbean climate.

As you savor each dish and explore the local specialties, you'll not only taste the flavors of Barbados but also gain a deeper understanding of the island's history, culture, and people.

Barbados Seafood Delicacies

This island's culinary landscape is adorned with a plethora of marine delights, each dish telling a story of the sea's bounty and the island's deep connection to it. Here are some of Barbados' seafood delicacies that will captivate your taste buds:

1. Grilled Marlin: Sink your teeth into the smoky allure of grilled marlin. Marlin steaks, marinated with a medley of herbs and spices, are expertly charred to create a masterpiece that's both succulent and flavorful. The smokiness complements the natural richness of the marlin, delivering a culinary experience that's both elegant and indulgent.

2. Sea Urchin Salad: For the adventurous palate, sea urchin salad offers a delicate and unique experience. Creamy sea urchin roe is combined with fresh ingredients like citrus, herbs, and perhaps a touch of olive oil, resulting in a dish that's as visually appealing as it is delectable.

3. Lobster Alive: Indulge in the decadence of lobster at its freshest at "Lobster Alive," where the seafood is not only prepared with precision but also captures the essence of the Caribbean. Savor the succulent lobster meat in various forms, from grilled to butter-poached, all while enjoying the laid-back ambiance of this beachfront eatery.

4. Seafood Roti: Experience the fusion of Indian and Caribbean flavors with seafood roti. A warm and flaky roti is generously filled with a mixture of curried seafood, including shrimp and fish, along with a medley of vegetables and fragrant spices. It's a comfort dish that's bursting with vibrant flavors.

5. Coconut-Crusted Shrimp: Satisfy your craving for a crunchy delight with coconut-crusted shrimp. These succulent morsels are coated in a delicate layer of grated coconut and breadcrumbs before being fried to golden perfection. The contrast between the crispy exterior and the tender shrimp within is a true culinary delight.

6. Seafood Cou-Cou: Cou-Cou, a beloved Barbadian dish, takes on a seafood twist in this preparation. Imagine a bed of creamy cou-cou adorned with a flavorful medley of shrimp, crab, and perhaps even a touch of lobster. The dish captures the heart of Bajan cuisine while embracing the bounty of the sea.

7. Seafood Chowder: Warm your soul with a bowl of hearty seafood chowder. Laden with a variety of seafood treasures such as fish, shrimp, and mussels, this comforting soup is often enriched with coconut milk and fragrant herbs. The result is a harmonious blend of flavors that epitomizes the island's culinary diversity.

8. Salt Fish and Bakes: Delight in the perfect union of salted fish and bakes—fluffy, deep-fried dough that's often enjoyed as a breakfast or snack. The salted fish is typically cod that has been rehydrated and cooked with onions, peppers, and aromatic seasonings, creating a flavorful filling for the bakes.

9. Smoked Tuna Dip: Dive into the delightful flavors of smoked tuna dip. A creamy mixture of smoked tuna, mayonnaise, herbs, and spices is served with crispy crackers or fresh vegetables. It's a light and satisfying appetizer that beautifully captures the essence of Barbados' coastal cuisine.

10. Mahi-Mahi Escabeche: Experience a burst of tangy flavors with mahi-mahi escabeche. This dish features lightly seared mahi-

mahi fillets marinated in a zesty mixture of vinegar, onions, bell peppers, and other aromatics. The marination process infuses the fish with vibrant flavors, creating a refreshing and delightful taste.

As you indulge in these seafood delicacies, you'll embark on a culinary adventure that showcases Barbados' deep-rooted connection to the sea, while embracing the island's creativity and cultural influences

Best Restaurants And Cafes In Barbados

Whether you're looking for a fine dining experience or a casual spot to grab a bite, Barbados has something to offer for every taste and budget.

The Cliff

The Cliff is a renowned fine dining restaurant located on the west coast of Barbados. The restaurant is perched on a cliff overlooking the ocean, providing diners with a breathtaking view. The cuisine is modern Caribbean with a focus on seafood, and the menu changes seasonally. Expect to pay around $100-$150 USD per person for dinner.

Tides

Tides is another popular fine dining restaurant located on the west coast of Barbados. The restaurant is housed in a beautifully restored historic building, and the cuisine is a fusion of Caribbean and Mediterranean flavors. The menu features fresh seafood, grilled meats, and vegetarian options. Expect to pay around $80-$120 USD per person for dinner.

Oistins Fish Fry

Oistins Fish Fry is a must-visit spot for seafood lovers. The fish fry takes place every Friday night in the town of Oistins, and it's a lively event that attracts both locals and tourists. You can sample a variety of fresh seafood, such as grilled fish, shrimp, and lobster, at affordable prices. Expect to pay around $15-$25 USD per person for dinner.

Champers

Champers is a casual yet elegant restaurant located on the south coast of Barbados. The restaurant is situated on a cliff overlooking the ocean, and it has a relaxed atmosphere. The cuisine is a fusion of Caribbean and international flavors, and the menu features fresh seafood, pasta dishes, and meat options. Expect to pay around $50-$80 USD per person for dinner.

Brown Sugar Restaurant

Brown Sugar Restaurant is a popular spot for tourists who want to sample traditional Bajan cuisine. The restaurant is located on the outskirts of Bridgetown, and it has a cozy atmosphere. The menu features dishes such as flying fish, macaroni pie, and cou-cou, which are all staples of Bajan cuisine. Expect to pay around $30-$50 USD per person for dinner.

Cuz's Fish Stand

Cuz's Fish Stand is a hidden gem located in Bridgetown. It's a no-frills spot that serves some of the best fish sandwiches on the island. The fish is fresh and seasoned to perfection, and the sandwiches are served on soft buns with lettuce and tomato. Expect to pay around $5-$10 USD per sandwich.

Coffee Barbados

Coffee Barbados is a popular coffee shop located in the heart of Bridgetown. The shop serves specialty coffee made from beans sourced from all over the world, and the menu features a variety of espresso drinks, pour-overs, and cold brews. There are also pastries and sandwiches available. Expect to pay around $4-$7 USD for a coffee.

Buzo Osteria Italiana

Buzo Osteria Italiana is a cozy Italian restaurant located in the Holetown area. The restaurant has an intimate atmosphere, and the menu features classic Italian dishes such as pasta, pizza, and risotto. There are also vegetarian and gluten-free options available. Expect to pay around $40-$70 USD per person for dinner.

The Village Cafe

The Village Cafe is a laid-back spot located in Holetown. The cafe serves breakfast, lunch, and dinner, and the menu features a variety of dishes such as sandwiches, salads, and burgers. There are also vegetarian and gluten-free options available. Expect to pay around $10-$20 USD per person for a meal.

Patisserie and Bistro Flindt

Patisserie and Bistro Flindt is a Danish bakery and restaurant located in the Limegrove Lifestyle Centre in Holetown. The bakery serves freshly baked bread, pastries, and cakes, while the restaurant offers a mix of European and Caribbean cuisine. There are also vegetarian and gluten-free options available. Expect to pay around $20-$40 USD per person for a meal.

Nishi Restaurant

Nishi Restaurant is a Japanese restaurant located in the Holetown area. The restaurant has a sleek and modern design, and the menu features classic Japanese dishes such as sushi, sashimi, and tempura. There are also vegetarian and gluten-free options available. Expect to pay around $50-$80 USD per person for dinner.

The Mews

The Mews is a trendy restaurant located in the heart of Holetown. The restaurant has an eclectic and stylish interior, and the menu features a mix of European and Caribbean cuisine. There are also vegetarian and gluten-free options available. Expect to pay around $50-$80 USD per person for dinner.

Carizma on the Hill

Carizma on the Hill is a fine dining restaurant located in the St. James area. The restaurant has a stunning panoramic view of the west coast, and the menu features a mix of European and Caribbean cuisine. The restaurant is also known for its extensive wine list. Expect to pay around $70-$100 USD per person for dinner.

Cafe Sol Mexican Grill and Margarita Bar

Cafe Sol Mexican Grill and Margarita Bar is a popular spot located in the St. Lawrence Gap area. The restaurant has a colorful and festive interior, and the menu features classic Mexican dishes such as tacos, burritos, and fajitas. The restaurant is also known for its delicious margaritas. Expect to pay around $20-$40 USD per person for a meal.

Just Grillin

Just Grillin is a casual restaurant chain with multiple locations around the island. The menu features grilled meats, seafood, and vegetarian options, as well as sides and salads. Expect to pay around $15-$30 USD per person for a meal.

Barbados is home to many restaurants and cafes that serve a wide range of cuisine at different price points. From fine dining to casual spots, there's something for everyone to enjoy. Whether you're a seafood lover or want to try traditional Bajan cuisine, Barbados has plenty to offer.

Bars And Nightlife

Here's a glimpse into the bars and nocturnal wonders that await you in this Caribbean paradise:

1. Harbour Lights: Step into the lively world of Harbour Lights, a beachfront hotspot that effortlessly blends Caribbean charm with electrifying energy. Sink your feet into the sand, feel the sea breeze, and dance to the rhythm of live music, soca, and calypso beats. This open-air club hosts themed beach parties, fire performances, and delectable cocktails that keep the spirits high long into the night.

2. Red Door Lounge: Unveil the secrets hidden behind the Red Door Lounge, a speakeasy-style establishment that exudes an air of mystery and sophistication. Tucked away in St. Lawrence Gap, this hidden gem invites you to enter a world of craft cocktails, sultry jazz, and an ambiance that transports you to a bygone era of clandestine revelry.

3. Priva Barbados: For a touch of luxury and exclusivity, Priva Barbados offers an upscale clubbing experience. With a focus on high-end cocktails and VIP service, this chic establishment caters to those who seek a more refined nightlife experience. The sleek design, pulsating beats, and stylish crowd create an ambiance that's both alluring and unforgettable.

4. The Mews Bar and Restaurant: Nestled in a historic building, The Mews Bar and Restaurant offers an elegant blend of dining and nightlife. Begin your evening with a gourmet meal in the cozy restaurant before transitioning to the bar area, where live music and a wide selection of wines and cocktails await. The intimate setting and eclectic decor add to the charm.

5. Baxters Road: Venture to Baxters Road for a taste of authentic Bajan nightlife. This lively street comes alive in the evening with a myriad of rum shops and street vendors. Join the locals in enjoying the sounds of reggae and soca, while sipping on rum and indulging in traditional street food like fried fish and cutters.

6. Copacabana Beach Bar: As the name suggests, Copacabana Beach Bar transports you to a tropical paradise of fun and relaxation. Located on Carlisle Bay, this vibrant bar offers a beachfront setting, inviting you to unwind on sunbeds while enjoying refreshing cocktails. The lively atmosphere, water sports, and friendly vibes make it a perfect daytime-to-nighttime spot.

7. John Moore Bar: Tucked away on the northwestern coast of Barbados, John Moore Bar is a rustic treasure where simplicity is celebrated. The bar overlooks the picturesque Half Moon Bay, providing a serene backdrop for sipping on a Banks beer or a rum punch while watching the sun set over the Caribbean Sea.

8. Surfer's Bay Beach Bar: If you're seeking a laid-back atmosphere, Surfer's Bay Beach Bar beckons. This eclectic beachfront bar is a haven for surfers and beach lovers alike. Enjoy live music, art exhibitions, and a diverse menu that celebrates local ingredients. Relax in a hammock, dip your toes in the sand, and let the waves and music carry you away.

As the night unfolds in Barbados, you'll discover that the island's nightlife isn't just about the drinks and music—it's a fusion of cultures, a celebration of life, and a chance to connect with both locals and fellow travelers.

Dinning Etiquette For Visitors

Here are some dining etiquette tips to keep in mind as a visitor:

1. Dress Appropriately: While Barbados is known for its laid-back atmosphere, dressing appropriately for dining is important. Many restaurants, especially upscale ones, have dress codes that may require you to wear smart-casual attire. Avoid beachwear or overly casual clothing when dining at more formal establishments.

2. Make Reservations: If you plan to dine at popular or upscale restaurants, making reservations is recommended, especially during peak tourist seasons. This ensures you have a spot and avoids disappointment due to high demand.

3. Punctuality: Arrive on time for your reservations, as punctuality is appreciated. It's a sign of respect for the restaurant and other guests.

4. Greetings: Upon entering the restaurant, greet the staff with a warm "good evening" or "hello." Polite interactions create a welcoming atmosphere.

5. Wait for Seating: Wait to be seated by the host or hostess, even if you've made a reservation. Seating arrangements are often organized to ensure the smooth flow of service.

6. Table Manners: Barbadian dining manners are generally in line with Western etiquette. Keep your elbows off the table, chew with your mouth closed, and use utensils appropriately. Wait for everyone at the table to be served before starting your meal.

7. Tipping: Tipping is customary in Barbados. Many restaurants include a service charge, but it's still common to leave an additional tip of around 10-15% if service was exceptional. Check the bill to see if a service charge has already been added.

8. Handling the Bill: When the meal is finished, the bill will be brought to the table. If you're ready to pay, signal to the server by placing your credit card or cash on the bill. It's not customary to rush diners out, so take your time to settle the bill.

9. Dietary Restrictions: If you have dietary restrictions or allergies, it's best to inform the restaurant staff when making the reservation or upon arrival. They will usually accommodate your needs to the best of their ability.

10. Conversation and Gratuity: Engaging in friendly conversation with staff is welcomed, as Barbadians are known for their warm hospitality. When leaving, express your gratitude with a friendly "thank you" to your server and other staff members who attended to you.

11. Enjoy the Local Cuisine: Barbadian cuisine is a delightful blend of flavors, so be open to trying local dishes and specialties. Embrace the opportunity to savor the island's culinary heritage.

By being mindful of these dining etiquette tips, you'll not only show respect for the local customs but also enhance your overall dining experience in Barbados.

CHAPTER FIVE

Top Landmarks And Attractions To Visit

There are a wide variety of attractions and activities for visitors to enjoy while exploring this beautiful island. Here are some of the top attractions in Barbados.

One of the most popular attractions in Barbados is the beautiful Harrison's Cave. This natural wonder is a series of underground caves that are home to stunning stalactites and stalagmites, crystal-clear streams, and underground pools. Visitors can take a guided tram tour through the caves to learn about the geological history of the island and the fascinating formations that make up the cave system.

Another popular attraction in Barbados is the beautiful coastline. The island boasts over 70 miles of pristine beaches, each with its own unique character and charm. The famous Crane Beach, located on the southeastern coast of the island, is known for its soft pink sand and crystal-clear waters. The beach is surrounded by rocky cliffs and lush vegetation, making it the perfect place to relax and soak up the sun.

For history buffs, the Barbados Museum and Historical Society is a must-visit attraction. Housed in a beautiful 19th-century military prison, the museum features exhibits that tell the story of Barbados' rich history, from its colonial past to its present-day culture. Visitors can learn about the island's sugar industry, the slave trade, and the island's role in the American Revolution.

Animal lovers will enjoy a visit to the Barbados Wildlife Reserve. This open-air park is home to a variety of exotic animals, including green monkeys, peacocks, and deer. Visitors can stroll through the park and observe the animals in their natural habitats, or take part in a feeding session to get up close and personal with the animals.

For those seeking adventure, a visit to the Andromeda Botanic Gardens is a must. This beautiful botanical garden is home to over six acres of tropical flora and fauna, including rare and exotic plants from around the world. Visitors can take a guided tour of the gardens to learn about the different plant species and their medicinal properties.

Finally, no trip to Barbados would be complete without a taste of the island's famous rum. Visitors can take a tour of the Mount Gay Rum Distillery, the oldest rum distillery in the world, to learn about the history of rum production on the island and how it has become a part of Barbadian culture. Visitors can also sample a variety of rum cocktails and purchase bottles of rum to take home as souvenirs.

Harrison Cave

Harrison Cave, a geological wonder sculpted over eons, stands as a testament to the captivating forces of nature and offers visitors a once-in-a-lifetime opportunity to explore its intricate formations, subterranean waterways, and awe-inspiring chambers. Embarking on a journey to Harrison Cave is not just a visit; it's an enchanting voyage into the heart of Earth's hidden treasures.

Upon arriving at the entrance of Harrison Cave, visitors are greeted by an air of excitement and anticipation. The cave's exterior resembles a mystical portal to another world, its facade adorned with vibrant tropical foliage and intriguing rock formations, hinting at the captivating beauty that lies beneath the surface. As guests descend into the cave, the temperature gently drops, creating an atmosphere that ignites curiosity and heightens the senses.

The grandeur of Harrison Cave becomes fully apparent as visitors step into the Cathedral Room, a magnificent chamber adorned with soaring stalactites and stalagmites that have been meticulously sculpted over millennia. The interplay of light and shadow creates an ethereal dance, casting an otherworldly glow on the calcite formations. The guide's narration weaves stories of geological processes and folklore, enhancing the experience with layers of knowledge and cultural richness.

The tour continues, revealing one marvel after another. The Great Hall showcases a tapestry of flowstone formations that resemble frozen waterfalls, suspended in time. As droplets of water trickle down the intricate formations, visitors are reminded of the ongoing dance between water and rock that has shaped these remarkable structures. The reflective pools that have formed over time mirror the formations above, doubling the visual splendor and adding an element of enchantment.

Harrison Cave is not just a static entity; it's a living, breathing system. The cave's waterways carve their paths through the limestone, forming underground rivers and streams. The Adventure Tour offers a chance to traverse these waterways on a tram-like vehicle, providing an intimate view of the cave's geological processes in action. The clear waters glisten under carefully positioned lights, revealing the intricate patterns etched into the cave walls and giving visitors a unique perspective on the dynamic relationship between water and rock.

Amidst the grandeur of the cave's formations, the eco-systems that have developed within Harrison Cave come into focus. The various chambers host delicate ecosystems that have adapted to the cave's unique environment. Explorers may catch a glimpse of cave-dwelling creatures, such as bats and crickets, which have carved their niche within this subterranean realm. The cave's protective environment plays a crucial role in preserving these rare and fascinating species.

For those seeking a more immersive experience, the Eco-Adventure Tour offers an opportunity to journey even deeper into the cave's unexplored passages. Equipped with headlamps and an adventurous spirit, participants crawl and climb through narrow passages, channeling their inner explorers. This intimate encounter with the cave's raw beauty is a testament to the hidden mysteries that lie beneath the surface, waiting to be uncovered by those willing to embark on a daring escapade.

As the tour concludes and visitors ascend back into the tropical daylight, the memories of Harrison Cave linger like a vivid dream. The cave's intricate formations, subterranean waterways, and awe-inspiring chambers weave together a tapestry of geological marvels that continue to evolve even as time marches on. The experience of exploring Harrison Cave isn't just about sightseeing; it's about embracing the earth's ancient past, understanding its geological processes, and fostering a deep connection to the natural world.

Harrison Cave in Barbados stands as a true testament to the wonders that nature can create over time. Its intricate formations, hidden chambers, and underground rivers tell a story that spans millions of years, inviting visitors to become a part of this narrative.

Nicholas Abbey

This enchanting estate, with its captivating colonial charm and serene surroundings, offers visitors a captivating journey through time, allowing them to immerse themselves in the rich heritage of the island. From the moment you step onto the cobblestone pathways that wind through the estate, you're transported to a bygone era, where the whispers of history intertwine with the rustling leaves and the gentle Caribbean breeze.

As you approach the grand entrance of Nicholas Abbey, the sight of the iconic Jacobean-style mansion greets you with its coral stone walls, elegant chimneys, and white gingerbread trim. Dating back to the 17th century, the architecture is a testament to the island's colonial past, and every stone seems to have a story to tell. The mansion, with its charming wooden shutters and commanding presence, stands as a guardian of Barbados' heritage.

Stepping inside, you're welcomed by a sense of timelessness. The interior of Nicholas Abbey exudes an air of opulence and nostalgia, with period furniture, vintage tapestries, and delicate porcelain reflecting the lifestyle of a bygone era. The Great House offers a glimpse into the lives of those who once inhabited this splendid estate, and every room holds the secrets of centuries past. The grand dining hall, the drawing room adorned with ancestral portraits, and the library filled with weathered books, all contribute to the immersive experience.

One of the highlights of a visit to Nicholas Abbey is the chance to witness the art of traditional sugar production. The estate boasts a fully operational sugar mill, a rare gem in today's world. As you stand before the towering windmill, you can almost hear the echoes of the past, when the rhythmic creaking and turning of its blades were the heartbeat of the plantation. The guided tour takes you through the step-by-step process of sugar production, from the pressing of sugarcane to the boiling of syrup in huge copper cauldrons. The aroma of molasses and the clinking of machinery evoke a sense of authenticity, as if you've stepped into a living history book.

The journey doesn't end there. Beyond the sugar mill lies a boundless tropical paradise. The Abbey's lush gardens sprawl across the landscape, offering a haven of serenity and natural beauty. The carefully landscaped gardens are a testament to the estate's commitment to preserving its environment, and every turn leads to a new discovery. The tropical flora and fauna create a symphony of colors and fragrances that enchant the senses. Stroll through the fragrant spice garden, where cinnamon and nutmeg trees stand as reminders of the island's spice-rich past. Pause by the tranquil lily pond, where koi fish glide beneath the surface, and breathe in the tranquility that envelops you.

For those seeking a moment of reflection, the tranquility of the plantation's mahogany forest provides an ideal escape. Towering mahogany trees create a natural cathedral of shade, where dappled sunlight filters through the leaves, illuminating the forest floor like scattered jewels. It's easy to lose track of time here, as the gentle rustling of leaves and the chorus of birds transport you to a realm of nature's beauty.

Before bidding farewell to Nicholas Abbey, a visit to the charming gift shop is a must. Here, you'll find a curated selection of locally crafted goods, including artisanal rum, delicate ceramics, and intricate lacework. These treasures serve as reminders of your journey through this enchanting estate, allowing you to carry a piece of Barbados' history and spirit back home with you.

Bridge Town

A visit to Bridgetown promises an immersive experience that seamlessly blends the island's colonial past with its modern flair, creating an enchanting tapestry of culture, adventure, and relaxation.

Historical Elegance: As you step into Bridgetown, you'll be transported back in time by the elegant remnants of its colonial history. The city's UNESCO-listed Garrison area boasts a fascinating collection of 17th-century buildings and fortifications, offering a glimpse into Barbados' role in shaping Caribbean history. Among the highlights is the impressive George Washington House, where a young George Washington once resided, giving visitors an unexpected connection to American history. The Barbados Museum, housed within a former British military prison, delves into the island's heritage through exhibits that span Amerindian artifacts, colonial relics, and tales of sugar barons.

Colorful Markets and Vibrant Culture: Bridgetown's bustling markets are a testament to the island's lively culture. The Careenage, a scenic waterfront area lined with colorful buildings, hosts the Cheapside Market, where local vendors proudly display a vivid array of fresh fruits, vegetables, spices, and crafts. A visit here is not only a chance to engage with the locals but also to immerse yourself in the vibrant tapestry of island life. Don't forget to sample the island's iconic dish, flying fish, which is often prepared with a medley of Caribbean spices and served with sides that celebrate the bounty of the sea.

Scenic Coastal Beauty: Barbados is renowned for its pristine beaches and Bridgetown is no exception. Brownes Beach, conveniently located near the city center, boasts powdery white sands and crystal-clear waters, making it the perfect spot to unwind and soak up the sun. If you're feeling adventurous, take to the waters for some snorkeling or even try your hand at surfing, an activity that Barbados is famous for.

Enchanting Architecture: Walking through the streets of Bridgetown is like embarking on a journey through architectural elegance. The Parliament Buildings, constructed from coral limestone, exhibit neo-Gothic design elements that contrast beautifully with the tropical surroundings. The historic St. Michael's Cathedral, with its intricate stained glass windows and towering spires, stands as a testament to the island's deep religious roots.

Harbor Adventure: Bridgetown's picturesque harbor serves as a gateway to maritime adventures. Catamaran cruises offer a chance to sail along the coast, taking in panoramic views of the city's skyline and the azure Caribbean waters. These cruises often include snorkeling excursions, providing an opportunity to explore the island's vibrant underwater ecosystem, replete with colorful coral formations and a dazzling array of marine life.

Festivals and Celebrations: For those fortunate enough to visit during the annual Crop Over Festival, Bridgetown transforms into a vibrant carnival of color, music, and dance. This traditional harvest festival celebrates Barbadian culture with parades, calypso competitions, and lively street parties. The infectious energy of the festivities is sure to leave you captivated and uplifted.

Connect with Locals: The warmth of the Barbadian people is a defining feature of Bridgetown. Engaging with the locals allows you to uncover the true heart of the island. Whether you're striking up a conversation with a fisherman along the pier or participating in a cooking class to learn the secrets of Bajan cuisine, these interactions will create lasting memories and a deeper appreciation for the island's culture.

Barbados Wildlife Reserve

Barbados Wildlife Reserve is a fascinating open-air park that offers visitors a chance to observe a variety of exotic animals in their natural habitats. The reserve is located on the island's northern edge, nestled within a beautiful mahogany forest, and covers an area of four acres.

One of the main attractions of the Barbados Wildlife Reserve is the green monkeys that roam freely throughout the park. These playful primates are native to Barbados and are known for their distinctive bright green color. Visitors can observe the monkeys as they swing through the trees, playfully interact with each other, and forage for food.

In addition to the green monkeys, the reserve is also home to a variety of other animals, including deer, iguanas, tortoises, and peacocks. Visitors can stroll through the park at their leisure, observing the animals as they interact with each other and their environment.

The park's enclosure for iguanas is particularly interesting, as it allows visitors to get up close and personal with these fascinating reptiles. Visitors can watch as the iguanas bask in the sun, climb trees, and engage in other natural behaviors.

One of the most impressive animals in the reserve is the Barbados agouti, a large rodent that is found only on the island. These animals are known for their distinctive black and white stripes and their elusive nature, as they are often difficult to spot in the wild. However, visitors to the reserve have a good chance of seeing these fascinating creatures in their natural habitat.

Another interesting feature of the Barbados Wildlife Reserve is its collection of birds. The park is home to a variety of exotic species, including parrots, macaws, and flamingos. Visitors can observe these colorful birds as they preen themselves, interact with each other, and feed.

The reserve is also home to a number of tortoises, including the giant tortoise. Visitors can observe these majestic creatures as they slowly make their way through the park, grazing on grass and other vegetation.

One of the most unique features of the Barbados Wildlife Reserve is its nocturnal house. This darkened enclosure is home to a variety of animals that are active at night, including bats, owls, and snakes. Visitors can observe these fascinating creatures as they go about their nighttime activities, providing a unique perspective on the park's animal inhabitants.

Throughout the park, visitors will encounter knowledgeable guides who are happy to answer questions and provide insights into the animals' behavior and natural habitats. The park also hosts regular feeding sessions, which provide an opportunity for visitors to see the animals up close and learn about their dietary needs.

Overall, the Barbados Wildlife Reserve is a fascinating destination that offers a unique glimpse into the island's diverse animal population. Whether you're interested in observing the green monkeys, getting up close and personal with iguanas, or marveling at the beauty of the park's bird species, the reserve is a must-visit attraction for anyone interested in nature and wildlife.

For visitors interested in exploring the park in greater depth, guided tours are available. These tours provide a deeper insight into the park's animals, their natural habitats, and the challenges they face in the wild. The guides are knowledgeable and passionate about the animals, and their enthusiasm is contagious.

Beaches And Coastal Areas

The island boasts over 60 miles of coastline, which is dotted with a range of beaches, bays, and cliffs. Whether you're looking for a relaxing day in the sun or an adventurous water-based activity, Barbados has something to offer for everyone.

One of the most popular beaches on the island is Crane Beach, located on the southeast coast of the island. The beach is famous for its turquoise waters and soft, pink sand, which makes it a popular destination for swimming and sunbathing. Visitors can also enjoy water sports such as surfing, boogie boarding, and snorkeling. The beach is backed by a beautiful cliff face, which provides a stunning backdrop for photos.

Another popular beach on the island is Accra Beach, located on the south coast. The beach is a popular destination for families, thanks to its calm waters and soft sand. Visitors can rent beach chairs and umbrellas, and enjoy a range of activities such as beach volleyball, jet skiing, and paddleboarding. The beach is also home to a range of restaurants and bars, making it a great place to grab a bite to eat or a refreshing drink.

For visitors looking for a more secluded beach experience, Bottom Bay is a great choice. The beach is located on the southeast coast of the island and is known for its picturesque setting. The beach is backed by steep cliffs and is surrounded by lush vegetation, making it a beautiful spot for a picnic or a relaxing day in the sun. Visitors can also enjoy swimming and snorkeling in the crystal-clear waters.

For those looking for a more rugged coastal experience, Bathsheba is a must-visit destination. The town is located on the east coast of the island and is renowned for its wild, untamed beauty. The rugged coastline is home to a range of rock formations and tide pools, which are great for exploring. The area is also a popular spot for surfing, thanks to its large waves and consistent swells.

For visitors looking for a more upscale beach experience, the west coast of the island is the place to be. The area is home to a range of luxurious resorts and high-end restaurants, making it a popular destination for the rich and famous. The beaches on the west coast are also known for their calm waters and soft sand, making them a great destination for swimming and sunbathing. Some of the most popular beaches on the west coast include Sandy Lane Beach and Mullins Beach.

One of the most unique coastal destinations on the island is the Animal Flower Cave, located on the north coast of the island. The cave is named after the sea anemones that can be found in the tidal pools located within the cave. Visitors can explore the cave and its tidal pools, which provide a unique glimpse into the island's geological history. The cave is also located on a cliff overlooking the ocean, providing stunning views of the coastline.

For visitors looking to explore the island's marine life, a snorkeling or scuba diving excursion is a must. Barbados is home to a range of colorful fish and marine creatures, as well as a number of shipwrecks and coral reefs. Some of the most popular snorkeling and diving spots on the island include Carlisle Bay, Folkestone Marine Park, and the Stavronikita wreck.

In addition to its beaches and coastal areas, Barbados is also home to a range of offshore islands and cays. These islands provide a unique opportunity to explore the island's natural beauty and marine life. Some of the most popular offshore destinations include the Grenadines, the Tobago Cays, and the Virgin Islands.

Marine Life And Coral Reefs

The coral reefs surrounding Barbados are some of the most extensive and diverse in the Caribbean. These reefs provide important habitats for a wide range of marine life, including fish, crustaceans, mollusks, and other invertebrates. The coral reefs are also a vital source of food for many local communities and support a thriving tourism industry.

Barbados has several marine protected areas that help to conserve the island's coral reefs and marine life. The Folkestone Marine Park and Reserve, located on the west coast of the island, is one of the most popular marine parks in Barbados. The park covers an area of approximately 2.2 square kilometers and is home to a wide range of marine species.

The coral reefs in the park are particularly impressive, with colorful coral formations providing important habitats for a variety of fish and other marine creatures. Visitors to the park can explore the coral reefs through snorkeling and scuba diving, observing the marine life up close and personal.

One of the most fascinating creatures that can be found in the waters surrounding Barbados is the sea turtle. These ancient reptiles are a common sight in the island's waters, particularly during the nesting season from March to October. Barbados is home to two species of sea turtles, the hawksbill and the green turtle.

The hawksbill turtle is particularly important to the island's marine ecosystem, as it feeds on the sponges that grow on the coral reefs.

These sponges can be harmful to the coral, so the hawksbill turtle plays a vital role in keeping the coral reefs healthy.

In addition to sea turtles, the waters around Barbados are home to a variety of other marine creatures, including colorful fish, rays, and sharks. The island's marine ecosystem also supports a thriving fishing industry, with local fishermen catching a variety of fish, including flying fish, marlin, and snapper.

Despite the importance of Barbados' coral reefs and marine life, these ecosystems face a variety of threats. One of the biggest threats is climate change, which is causing rising sea temperatures and ocean acidification. These changes can cause coral bleaching, which can be fatal to the coral reefs and the marine creatures that depend on them.

Overfishing and pollution are also major threats to Barbados' marine ecosystem. Overfishing can deplete fish populations, disrupting the delicate balance of the ecosystem. Pollution, including plastic waste and chemical runoff from agriculture, can harm marine life and damage the coral reefs.

To address these threats, the government of Barbados has implemented a variety of conservation measures. Marine protected areas, such as the Folkestone Marine Park and Reserve, are designed to conserve the island's coral reefs and marine life. The government has also implemented regulations on fishing and has launched campaigns to reduce pollution and plastic waste.

Tourism plays an important role in Barbados' economy, and the island's marine ecosystem is a major attraction for visitors. Many hotels and resorts offer snorkeling and scuba diving excursions, providing visitors with the opportunity to explore the island's coral reefs and observe the colorful marine life up close.

However, it's important for visitors to be mindful of their impact on the environment. Snorkelers and divers should be careful not to touch or disturb the coral reefs or marine life, as this can cause damage to the ecosystem. Visitors should also be mindful of their waste and should avoid littering or leaving plastic waste on the beach.

Caves And Underground Rivers

Barbados is known for its pristine beaches, lush forests, and vibrant culture. However, the island is also home to a series of stunning caves and underground rivers that offer visitors a unique and fascinating glimpse into the island's geology and natural history.

Harrison's Cave is one of the most popular underground attractions in Barbados. This cave system is located in the central part of the island and is accessible by tram. Visitors are taken through a series of caverns and tunnels, each with its own unique features, including waterfalls, pools, and stunning rock formations. The cave system is thought to be over a million years old and is believed to have been formed by the erosion of limestone.

Another popular cave system in Barbados is the Animal Flower Cave. This cave is located on the northern tip of the island and is named after the sea anemones that can be found in its rock pools. The cave features stunning views of the Atlantic Ocean, and visitors can even swim in its crystal-clear waters. The cave is thought to be over 400,000 years old and is believed to have been formed by the erosion of coral rock.

The Welchman Hall Gully is a unique attraction that combines the beauty of a tropical forest with the intrigue of underground caves. The gully is located in the center of the island and is home to a variety of plants and animals, including monkeys, iguanas, and tropical birds. Visitors can take a guided tour through the gully, which includes a visit to a series of underground caves that were formed by the erosion of limestone. These caves are home to a variety of stalactites and stalagmites, and visitors can observe the unique geological features that make this attraction so special.

The Crystal Cove is another popular underground attraction in Barbados. This cave is located on the southern coast of the island and is accessible by boat. Visitors can explore the cave's crystal-clear waters and marvel at the stunning rock formations that line its walls. The cave is thought to have been formed over thousands of years by the action of the sea.

The Earthworks Pottery is an interesting attraction that combines the beauty of underground caves with the artistry of pottery. The pottery is located on the northern edge of the island and features a series of underground caves that have been transformed into pottery workshops. Visitors can observe local artisans as they create unique pottery pieces using traditional techniques. The cave system is thought to be over 2 million years old and is believed to have been formed by the erosion of coral rock.

The Chalky Mount Potteries is another pottery attraction that is worth a visit. This pottery is located in the central part of the island and features a series of underground caves that have been transformed into pottery workshops. Visitors can observe local artisans as they create unique pottery pieces using traditional techniques. The cave system is thought to be over 1 million years old and is believed to have been formed by the erosion of coral rock.

From the stunning rock formations of Harrison's Cave to the crystal-clear waters of Crystal Cove, each of these attractions offers visitors a unique and memorable experience. Whether you're interested in exploring the island's geological history or simply looking for an interesting and educational experience, Barbados' caves and underground rivers are a must-see attraction.

CHAPTER SIX

Off-Road Adventure

While the beaches are enchanting, the heart of this island's allure lies in its rugged terrains, lush jungles, and untamed wilderness. Strap in, for we're about to dive into an off-road adventure that will make your heart race and your soul come alive.

Leave behind the bustling streets of Bridgetown and set your compass for the heart of Barbados' wilderness. As your off-road vehicle bounces to life, you'll feel a surge of excitement coursing through your veins. Wind through dense rainforests, where ancient trees reach for the heavens and vibrant birdsong echoes in the air.

Take the path less traveled – or perhaps, barely trodden – and you'll discover a labyrinth of trails that wind through rolling hills, rocky descents, and hidden valleys. The verdant landscape shifts around you, from sun-dappled clearings to shadowy ravines, each revealing a new facet of the island's wild beauty.

As you navigate through the ever-changing terrain, prepare to be amazed by Barbados' natural wonders. Ascend to panoramic viewpoints that will steal your breath, revealing the endless expanse of the azure Caribbean Sea stretching beyond the horizon. Challenge yourself as you conquer steep inclines and adrenaline-pumping descents, all while surrounded by a symphony of tropical sounds.

What truly makes this off-road adventure in Barbados exceptional is the chance to interact with the island's welcoming locals. Along your journey, encounter villages tucked away from the tourist trail. Immerse yourself in the rich Bajan culture, sharing stories with fishermen as they mend their nets and swapping laughter with farmers tending to their crops. It's these moments that paint an authentic picture of life on the island, allowing you to forge connections that will last a lifetime.

No adventure is complete without indulging in the local flavors. After an exhilarating day of off-road exploration, treat your taste buds to an array of mouthwatering Bajan dishes. Sample flying fish – the national dish – expertly prepared with an array of spices that dance on your palate. Wash it down with a refreshing glass of rum punch, the essence of Barbadian merriment captured in a single sip.

While you revel in the thrill of off-road adventure, remember that the landscapes you traverse are delicate ecosystems. Barbados prides itself on its commitment to eco-conscious tourism. Stick to designated trails, respecting the flora and fauna that call this island home. By leaving only tire tracks and taking only memories, you'll play a vital role in preserving this paradise for generations to come.

Village And Community Tours

For visitors who want to experience the local culture, a village and community tour is an excellent way to do so. These tours offer visitors the opportunity to explore local villages, meet local residents, and learn about the island's history and culture.

One of the best ways to experience village and community tours in Barbados is through a guided tour. These tours are typically led by local guides who are knowledgeable about the area and its history. They can provide visitors with a unique insight into the local culture and traditions, and help them to connect with the local community.

The tours can take visitors to a variety of different communities and villages, each with its own unique charm and character. One of the most popular tours is the Bridgetown Walking Tour, which takes visitors through the historic capital city of Bridgetown. The tour includes visits to historic sites such as the Parliament Buildings and the Garrison Savannah, as well as the local market, where visitors can experience the vibrant energy of the city.

Another popular tour is the Holetown Heritage Walking Tour, which takes visitors through the charming village of Holetown. This tour includes visits to historic sites such as St. James Church and the Holetown Monument, as well as a chance to explore the local shops and restaurants.

For visitors who want to experience the local culture in a more immersive way, homestay tours are a great option. These tours allow visitors to stay with local families and experience their way of life first-hand. Visitors can learn about local customs and traditions, and participate in activities such as cooking and farming.

In addition to these guided tours, visitors can also explore local communities on their own. Many villages and communities have local markets and events that visitors can attend, such as the Oistins Fish Fry, which takes place every Friday night. This event is a great opportunity to experience the local cuisine and culture, as visitors can sample fresh seafood and enjoy live music and entertainment.

Visitors can also explore local villages and communities by renting a car or taking a taxi. This allows them to explore at their own pace and discover hidden gems that might not be included on guided tours. Some popular villages to visit include Bathsheba, a picturesque fishing village on the east coast, and Speightstown, a charming town with a rich history and a vibrant local culture.

One of the benefits of village and community tours in Barbados is that they provide visitors with a deeper understanding of the island's history and culture. For example, visitors can learn about the island's history as a major sugar producer and its role in the transatlantic slave trade. They can also learn about the island's unique cultural traditions, such as the Crop Over Festival, which celebrates the end of the sugar cane harvest.

Overall, village and community tours in Barbados offer visitors a unique opportunity to experience the local culture and connect with the local community. Whether visitors choose to explore on their own or take a guided tour, they are sure to discover the rich history and traditions that make Barbados such a special place.

Historic Churches To Visit

Among its many historical treasures, the island's churches stand as enduring witnesses to the passage of time, reflecting the spiritual and cultural heritage of the Bajan people. Join me on a journey through the centuries as we uncover the stories and architectural marvels of some of Barbados' most historic churches.

St. John's Parish Church: A Testament to Resilience: Perched atop a cliff overlooking the Atlantic Ocean, St. John's Parish Church stands as a testament to the indomitable spirit of the Bajan people. Built in 1836 to replace an earlier structure destroyed by a hurricane, this Gothic masterpiece is a blend of coral stone and craftsmanship. The churchyard's gravestones tell stories of lives lived, loves lost, and generations that have passed, while the panoramic views from this vantage point remind visitors of the island's natural beauty and historical significance.

St. Nicholas Abbey: A Sanctuary of Elegance: While often referred to as an abbey, St. Nicholas Abbey is, in fact, an exquisite Jacobean mansion. Built in the 17th century, it is a rare example of this architectural style in the Western Hemisphere. The abbey's enchanting gardens, charming interior, and lush surroundings offer a glimpse into the lives of the island's plantation owners during colonial times. A visit here is like stepping back in time, as the abbey transports you to an era of grandeur and refined elegance.

St. James Parish Church: A Spiritual Haven: Nestled in the heart of Holetown, St. James Parish Church is one of the oldest churches on the island, dating back to the early 1600s. Its architecture is a blend of Gothic and Georgian influences, showcasing its historical evolution. The church's peaceful grounds and serene atmosphere offer visitors a place for reflection and contemplation, while its connection to the island's history as a former plantation church adds layers of cultural significance.

Christ Church Parish Church: A Symbol of Faith: Christ Church Parish Church, affectionately known as "The Church by the Sea," has been a beacon of faith for over three centuries. Its simple yet elegant design, adorned with coral stone and stained glass windows, exudes a sense of tranquility. The churchyard houses tombs of notable Bajans, including the island's only known Jacobean tombstone. The panoramic vista of the turquoise waters from this location makes it a place where spiritual and natural beauty seamlessly converge.

Museums And Galleries

Here are some noteworthy museums and galleries to visit in Barbados:

Barbados Museum and Historical Society: The Barbados Museum is housed in a former British military prison in Bridgetown, the capital city. It offers a comprehensive look into the island's history, including its indigenous people, African heritage, colonial past, and sugar industry. The museum features a diverse range of artifacts, exhibits, and interactive displays. Visitors can explore historical documents, maps, and art pieces. The museum also has beautiful gardens.

Opening Hours: Monday to Saturday, 9:00 AM - 5:00 PM

Admission Fee:

Adults: BDS $20 (about USD $10),

Children (ages 5-12): BDS $10 (about USD $5)

George Washington House and Museum: This museum is of significant historical importance, as it was the residence of a young George Washington during his visit to Barbados in 1751. The house provides insight into Washington's formative years and his interactions with the island's society. The museum features period furnishings, interactive displays, and exhibits about Washington's time on the island.

Opening Hours: Monday to Saturday, 9:00 AM - 4:30 PM

Admission Fee:

Adults: BDS $20 (about USD $10),

Children (ages 5-12): BDS $10 (about USD $5)

Arlington House Museum: Situated in Speightstown, Arlington House is a restored 18th-century building that offers a glimpse into Barbadian life during that era. The museum uses multimedia exhibits to illustrate the history of Speightstown, the island's second-largest town. Visitors can explore the interactive "Walk Through Time" exhibit and learn about the town's evolution.

Opening Hours: Monday to Saturday, 9:30 AM - 4:30 PM

Admission Fee:

Adults: BDS $25 (about USD $12.50),

Children (ages 5-12): BDS $12 (about USD $6)

Holder's House and Art Gallery: Holder's House, a historic plantation house, hosts an art gallery showcasing the works of both local and international artists. The gallery features paintings, sculptures, and ceramics. The surrounding gardens are also a treat to explore.

Opening Hours: Tuesday to Saturday, 10:00 AM - 4:00 PM

Admission Fee: Free

Lancaster Great House and Museum: This grand plantation house has been transformed into a museum that delves into Barbados' colonial history, particularly focusing on the sugar trade and plantation life. The museum displays antiques, historical artifacts, and a collection of military memorabilia.

Opening Hours: Monday to Friday, 9:00 AM - 4:00 PM

Admission Fee:

Adults: BDS $35 (about USD $17.50),

Children (ages 5-12): BDS $20 (about USD $10)

Please note that the information provided, including opening hours and admission fees, is based on my last visit to the region in November 2022. It's recommended to verify the details before planning your visit, as there may have been changes since then.

Cultural Festival And Event In Barbados

Barbados, a vibrant and culturally rich Caribbean island, hosts a diverse range of festivals and events throughout the year that celebrate its history, music, art, cuisine, and unique heritage. These festivals provide a unique opportunity for both locals and visitors to immerse themselves in the island's vibrant culture. Here are some of the most prominent cultural festivals and events in Barbados:

Crop Over Festival: The Crop Over Festival is one of Barbados' most iconic and longest-standing traditions. Originally rooted in the celebration of the sugar cane harvest, the festival has evolved into a vibrant showcase of Bajan culture. It spans several months, culminating in a grand finale known as Grand Kadooment Day. The festival features calypso and soca music, colorful costumes, lively street parades, art exhibitions, and traditional Bajan cuisine.

Date: Crop Over Festival typically starts in June and concludes with Grand Kadooment Day in early August.

Holetown Festival: Held in the historic town of Holetown, this week-long festival commemorates the island's first settlement in 1627. The festival includes live music performances, craft markets, historical reenactments, and a colorful street parade. It's a great opportunity to experience Barbados' rich history and community spirit.

Date: Typically held in February.

Oistins Fish Festival: As Barbados is surrounded by the sea, the Oistins Fish Festival pays homage to the island's fishing heritage. This event features a variety of seafood dishes, traditional Bajan games, live music, and a popular fish boning competition. It's a lively celebration of both culinary and cultural traditions.

Date: Usually held during the Easter weekend.

Holders Season: Held at the historic Holders House, this event is a showcase of world-class music, theater, and art. The festival attracts international performers and offers a range of performances, from classical music to contemporary dance and theatrical productions. The stunning backdrop of Holders House and its gardens adds to the charm of the experience.

Date: Events are spread out over several weeks from January to April.

Reggae Festival: Barbados' Reggae Festival is a celebration of Caribbean music and culture, featuring renowned reggae and dancehall artists from across the region. The festival includes live performances, parties, and beach concerts, all set against the backdrop of Barbados' beautiful beaches.

Date: Typically held in April or May.

Barbados Food and Rum Festival: This gastronomic event brings together local and international chefs, rum experts, and food enthusiasts. It showcases Barbados' culinary heritage, with cooking demonstrations, tasting events, and gourmet dining experiences. The festival highlights the island's renowned rum and diverse cuisine.

Date: Usually takes place in October.

Barbados Independent Film Festival: This film festival celebrates cinematic creativity from around the world. It showcases a diverse range of films, including feature films, documentaries, and short films. The festival includes screenings, workshops, and discussions with filmmakers.

Date: Typically held in January.

These are just a few examples of the many cultural festivals and events that take place in Barbados throughout the year.

CHAPTER SEVEN

Outdoor Adventure To Try Out

From its stunning beaches to its lush tropical forests and coral reefs, there is no shortage of exciting activities to explore.

One of the most popular outdoor activities in Barbados is snorkeling or scuba diving. The island's coral reefs are home to a variety of colorful marine life, including sea turtles, tropical fish, and even shipwrecks. Visitors can take guided tours or rent equipment to explore these underwater wonders.

Another great way to experience the natural beauty of Barbados is through hiking. The island has several scenic trails that lead through lush forests and past stunning waterfalls. One popular hike is the trail that leads to the top of Mount Hillaby, the highest point on the island, which offers breathtaking views of the surrounding landscape.

For those who prefer more adrenaline-fueled activities, Barbados also has opportunities for surfing, windsurfing, kiteboarding, and jet skiing. The island's consistent waves and steady trade winds make it an ideal destination for these high-energy sports.

Fishing And Boating

As the sun rises over the horizon, casting a golden hue upon the tranquil waters, fishing aficionados find themselves drawn to the vibrant fishing villages and marinas that dot the coastline. The island's rich maritime history comes alive as local fishermen set sail in their colorful wooden boats, their laughter carrying on the salty breeze. From the seasoned angler to the curious beginner, Barbados offers an array of fishing experiences to suit every taste.

For those who crave adventure, deep-sea fishing is an absolute must. Board a well-equipped fishing charter, where expert guides will lead you to the sparkling depths of the Caribbean Sea in search of big-game trophies. Feel the exhilaration as you battle mighty marlins, swift sailfish, and robust tunas, your heart racing as you grapple with these ocean giants. The thrill of reeling in a prized catch is an experience that will be etched in your memory forever.

If a more serene encounter with nature beckons, consider trying your hand at reef fishing. Set anchor near the vibrant coral reefs, where a plethora of colorful marine life awaits beneath the surface. Drop your line and watch as curious fish dart in and out of the coral formations, creating a mesmerizing aquatic ballet. The waters around Barbados are teeming with snappers, groupers, and barracudas, promising an unforgettable fishing expedition.

And let's not forget the joy of boating in Barbados, where the endless azure waters are your playground. Whether you're a skilled sailor or a casual explorer, you'll find the perfect vessel to suit your desires. Rent a sleek catamaran and let the wind carry you along the coastline, the rhythmic lapping of waves against the hull providing a soothing soundtrack. Discover hidden coves, remote beaches, and secret snorkeling spots, each more enchanting than the last.

As the sun dips below the horizon, casting a fiery palette of oranges and purples across the sky, you'll find that your fishing and boating adventures are only the beginning of the magic that Barbados has to offer. Indulge in the island's delectable cuisine, savoring the flavors of freshly caught seafood prepared with a Caribbean twist. Engage in lively conversations with locals, who will regale you with tales of maritime folklore and island traditions.

Golfing

Amidst this tropical splendor lies a golfing experience that transcends the ordinary, inviting visitors to indulge in a game that is as much about the breathtaking surroundings as it is about the sport itself.

Imagine stepping onto meticulously manicured fairways that seem to stretch out like emerald ribbons, each one framed by swaying palm trees and vibrant tropical blooms. As you make your way through the course, the gentle ocean breeze whispers secrets from afar, and the distant sound of waves crashing against the shore creates a soothing rhythm that accompanies your every swing.

The Royal Westmoreland Golf Course, a masterpiece designed by renowned architect Robert Trent Jones Jr., beckons golfing enthusiasts with its challenging layout and awe-inspiring views. Nestled within an exclusive estate, this par-72 course offers a harmonious blend of lush vegetation and dramatic elevation changes. Tee off amidst the lush vegetation and dramatic elevation changes as you navigate through 18 holes of pure golfing pleasure.

Breathtaking vistas await you at every turn – whether you're teeing off against the backdrop of the cerulean Caribbean Sea or sizing up your approach shot with the majestic St. James Parish Church in the distance. The scent of saltwater mingles with the earthy aroma of freshly cut grass, creating an olfactory symphony that captures the essence of Barbados itself.

As you make your way to the 19th hole, prepare to be enchanted by the warmth of Bajan hospitality. The elegant clubhouse stands as a testament to colonial architecture, where you can savor local delicacies and refreshing rum cocktails. Share stories of your best shots and near misses with fellow golfers from around the world, forging connections and friendships that transcend borders.

For those seeking an unparalleled golfing adventure, Apes Hill Club presents an irresistible challenge. Designed by course architect Chris Cole, this par-72 championship course seamlessly integrates natural rock formations, rolling hills, and dense tropical foliage into the game. As you conquer each hole, you'll find yourself in a constant dialogue with both nature and the game, testing your skills and strategic prowess.

Golfing in Barbados is not merely a sport; it's a sensory journey through a land of vivid colors, enchanting melodies, and invigorating challenges. Whether you're a seasoned golfer looking for your next great golf escape or a novice eager to experience the sport against a backdrop of unparalleled beauty, Barbados offers an extraordinary canvas on which to paint your golfing masterpiece.

Scuba Diving And Snorkeling

Nestled like a dazzling gem in the cerulean expanse of the Caribbean Sea, the enchanting island of Barbados beckons to adventurers and water enthusiasts with its aquatic wonders. Beneath the surface of its crystalline waters lies an aquatic wonderland that awaits eager explorers, offering a symphony of colors, textures, and marine life that beckons to be discovered. Whether you're a seasoned diver or a curious snorkeler, Barbados offers an underwater paradise that's bound to leave you breathless – in the best possible way.

Scuba Diving: A Journey into the Deep

For those who dare to venture into the depths of the ocean, Barbados offers a plethora of diving sites that cater to all skill levels. Imagine descending into the clear blue abyss, where vibrant coral reefs extend like underwater cities, and schools of tropical fish weave intricate patterns through the sunlight-dappled waters.

One of the crown jewels of Barbados' diving scene is the SS Stavronikita, a sunken freighter turned artificial reef. Sitting in the depths at around 120 feet, this wreck is a hauntingly beautiful testament to the ocean's power and the potential for rebirth. As you navigate the wreck's skeletal structure, you'll be joined by a mesmerizing array of marine life – from playful sea turtles to inquisitive barracudas – making it an experience that will linger in your memory.

The vibrant coral gardens of the Folkestone Marine Park are another underwater spectacle that divers won't want to miss. Here, you'll plunge into a kaleidoscope of colors as soft and hard corals stretch towards the surface, their intricate formations providing refuge to an astonishing diversity of marine creatures.

Snorkeling: A Dance with Shimmering Shallows

If diving isn't quite your forte, fear not, for Barbados also offers captivating snorkeling experiences that provide a glimpse into the underwater world without the need for specialized training. Wade into the shallows of the Carlisle Bay Marine Park, and you'll find yourself in a realm of stunning visibility where playful fish dart through the water just inches from your mask.

The aptly named Animal Flower Cave presents snorkelers with a unique opportunity to explore underwater caves, where sunlight filters through submerged entrances, casting an ethereal glow over the hidden wonders within. As you glide through these secret chambers, the gentle sway of the water adds a dreamlike quality to the experience.

Before embarking on your aquatic adventure, it's important to ensure that you're well-prepared. Local dive shops and tour operators offer a range of guided experiences for both scuba diving and snorkeling. If you're new to the world of scuba diving, certified instructors can guide you through the basics and ensure your safety as you explore the depths.

Remember to pack sunscreen, a hat, and plenty of water, as the tropical sun can be relentless, even when you're submerged in the ocean's embrace. And don't forget your underwater camera – you'll want to capture the stunning vistas and unforgettable encounters to relive them long after you've returned to dry land.

Skydiving And Paragliding

Barbados, a tropical haven known for its vibrant culture and breathtaking landscapes, unveils an exhilarating chapter of its story through the captivating experiences of skydiving and paragliding.

Skydiving: Dancing with Gravity

As the golden sun breaches the horizon, casting a warm embrace over the island, adrenaline pulses through your veins at the thought of a skydiving adventure in Barbados. The adventure begins at an airfield humming with excitement, where expert instructors guide you through the steps, transforming anticipation into unwavering determination.

The ascent aboard a small aircraft is a spectacle in itself. Gazing out of the window, you witness Barbados unfurl beneath you like a magnificent tapestry. The lush greenery, the pristine beaches, and the charming towns appear more like a painting than reality, and your heart races in sync with the propeller's rhythm.

At the threshold of the open door, with the wind's whispers in your ears and the distant waves serenading you, you step into the void. Time suspends as you plummet, defying gravity in a symphony of exhilaration and sensory overload. The world is a blur of colors and emotions as the wind whistles past, and the sense of freedom is indescribable.

Then, as if by magic, tranquility blankets you as the parachute deploys, offering a gentle embrace that slows your descent. Now, suspended above paradise, you have a front-row seat to Barbados' breathtaking panorama. The swaying palm trees, the rhythmic waves, and the vibrant culture all converge, etching an indelible memory that you'll carry forever.

Paragliding: A Ballet with the Wind

For those who seek the sky with a gentler touch, paragliding in Barbados offers an enchanting alternative. Imagine standing atop a rugged cliff, your heart synchronized with the rhythm of the waves below. The colorful canopy billows behind you, a promise of the journey that awaits.

With a surge of adrenaline, you launch into the air, and suddenly, you're part of a living canvas. The world below transforms into a mesmerizing mosaic: the cerulean sea embraces the coastline, verdant landscapes stretch like emerald blankets, and charming villages peek out from between the trees.

Guided by the breeze, you become one with the elements, an airborne ballet dancer. With gentle tugs and subtle shifts, you paint trails in the sky, weaving an intricate tapestry of flight. Every moment feels like an eternity, a symphony of tranquility punctuated by exhilaration.

Barbados, with its lush beauty and warm hospitality, sets the stage for these aerial escapades. But beyond the landscapes and adventures, it's the heart-pounding rhythm of life, the thrill of embracing the unknown, that defines the essence of skydiving and paragliding here.

Ziplining And Surfing

Barbados stands as an open invitation to those who seek an adrenaline-charged connection with both land and sea. Step away from the ordinary and dive into the extraordinary as you embark on exhilarating ziplining and surfing escapades that will forever etch the island's spirit into your soul.

Ziplining: A Skyward Symphony of Thrills

Picture yourself deep within the embrace of a dense tropical forest, where lush foliage stretches towards the heavens and curious wildlife watches your every move. Amidst this green sanctuary lies a network of ziplines that promise to unveil the island's natural beauty from an entirely new perspective. The journey begins with a climb to the treetops, where each platform stands as a gateway to a realm where gravity takes a backseat to excitement.

As you step onto the first platform, a cocktail of anticipation and awe courses through your veins. The tropical breeze tousles your hair as you push off into the void, and suddenly, you're soaring. The world beneath transforms into a vibrant tapestry of colors and shapes, while the sound of leaves rustling and distant waves crashing compose a symphony of sensations. Each zipline becomes a conduit for liberation, carrying you from one platform to the next, your heart pounding in time with the rhythm of adventure.

Between the exhilarating flights, suspension bridges beckon you to navigate narrow pathways that challenge your balance and heighten your senses. The verdant canopy envelops you, creating an intimate connection with the lush ecosystem that thrives beneath. With every step and every zip, Barbados unveils a new layer of itself – a hidden world that few have the privilege to explore.

Surfing: Riding the Caribbean's Heartbeat

From the heights of the forest canopy, your adventure descends to the vibrant embrace of the ocean. Barbados, known as a surfing mecca, boasts some of the most sought-after waves in the Caribbean. The island's coastline is a playground for both beginners and seasoned surfers, offering an opportunity to harmonize with the rhythm of the sea.

The iconic Bathsheba Beach beckons with its powerful waves and dramatic rock formations. Here, the surf schools cater to those taking their first steps on a board, patiently guiding you through the process of catching your first wave. As the sun paints the horizon with hues of gold and orange, you paddle out, your heart racing with excitement and a touch of trepidation. But as you feel the swell beneath you and the board responds to your commands, fear transforms into exhilaration. You're riding the very heartbeat of the Caribbean, a primal force that has sculpted these shores for millennia.

For the more experienced surfers, the Soup Bowl awaits – a world-renowned reef break that delivers a fast and hollow wave, challenging even the most adept riders. The thrill of dropping into a wave, feeling the power of the ocean beneath your feet, is a sensation that words struggle to encapsulate. It's a dance of balance and intuition, where you become one with the wave and the island's soul.

Hiking And Trekking

While many visitors flock to the island's stunning beaches, Barbados also offers a wealth of hiking and nature trails that showcase the island's lush forests, rolling hills, and stunning coastline.

Hiking in Barbados is a great way to explore the island's rugged terrain and immerse oneself in its natural beauty. There are several trails available, ranging from easy strolls to more challenging treks. The trails are well-maintained and marked, making them accessible to hikers of all skill levels.

One of the most popular hiking trails in Barbados is the Barbados Wildlife Reserve, located in the parish of St. Peter. The reserve is home to a variety of exotic animals, including monkeys, tortoises, and deer, as well as a wide range of bird species. The reserve's trails lead through lush tropical forests and past several natural water features, making it an ideal spot for nature lovers and hikers alike.

Another popular hiking destination is the Farley Hill National Park, located in the parish of St. Peter. The park offers several hiking trails that wind through its lush forests and past its historic ruins. Farley Hill is also home to a stunning view of the Atlantic Ocean, making it an ideal spot for nature photography and picnics.

For those looking for a more challenging hiking experience, the trail to the top of Mount Hillaby is a must-do. Mount Hillaby is the highest point on the island, reaching a height of 340 meters. The trail leading to the summit is steep and rugged, but the breathtaking views from the top make the climb well worth the effort.

The Scotland District, located in the parish of St. Andrew, is another excellent hiking destination. The district offers several trails that lead through its rolling hills and past its stunning gullies. The area is also home to several natural water features, including cascading waterfalls and crystal-clear streams.

In addition to hiking, Barbados also offers several nature trails that showcase the island's unique flora and fauna. One of the most popular nature trails is the Welchman Hall Gully, located in the parish of St. Thomas. The gully is a natural wonderland, home to over 200 species of tropical plants and trees. Visitors can take a guided tour or explore the gully on their own, following its winding trails past towering bamboo groves, flowering orchids, and towering palm trees.

Another popular nature trail is the Andromeda Botanic Gardens, located in the parish of St. Joseph. The gardens are home to a vast collection of tropical plants, including rare orchids and exotic palms. Visitors can take a leisurely stroll through the gardens, marveling at the stunning flowers and unique plant life.

For those looking for a more adventurous nature experience, the Animal Flower Cave, located in the parish of St. Lucy, is a must-see. The cave is home to several natural pools, including a crystal-clear underground lake. Visitors can take a guided tour of the cave, exploring its winding tunnels and marveling at its stunning rock formations.

Sustainable Tourism Practices

Beyond its beauty, the island is also a beacon of sustainable tourism, exemplifying how responsible practices can harmonize with nature and community, ensuring a brighter future for generations to come.

Preserving Natural Wonders

From the azure waters that hug the coastline to the verdant forests that thrive inland, Barbados recognizes the importance of safeguarding its natural wonders. The island's commitment to marine conservation is evident through protected areas that nurture delicate ecosystems, ensuring that coral reefs and marine life flourish undisturbed. Initiatives like coral restoration projects and efforts to reduce plastic waste showcase Barbados' dedication to preserving its marine habitats.

Community Engagement and Empowerment

Sustainable tourism extends beyond nature to the communities that call Barbados home. The island prioritizes engaging local communities, allowing visitors to experience the genuine warmth of Bajan culture. Locally-run accommodations, restaurants, and tours provide not only authentic experiences but also direct economic benefits to residents. By involving locals in the tourism industry, Barbados promotes community empowerment and an appreciation for the island's heritage.

Cultural Immersion and Education

Barbados is more than just a pretty postcard – it's a living testament to history and culture. Sustainable tourism practices prioritize educating visitors about the island's past, traditions, and way of life. Museums, heritage sites, and cultural festivals offer immersive experiences that foster a deep connection with Barbados' identity. Through these encounters, travelers gain a profound respect for the island's heritage and a commitment to its preservation.

Balanced Development

Barbados understands that maintaining the delicate balance between development and conservation is crucial. The island implements responsible planning and construction regulations to prevent overdevelopment that could harm the environment. By prioritizing sustainable infrastructure and architectural designs, Barbados ensures that its natural beauty remains unspoiled and its charm endures.

Renewable Energy and Conservation Efforts

As a testament to its commitment to sustainability, Barbados has made strides in adopting renewable energy sources. Solar power initiatives and energy-efficient practices in hotels and businesses contribute to reducing the island's carbon footprint. Moreover, Barbados' National Conservation Commission engages in reforestation efforts, ensuring that the island's lush landscapes remain vibrant and resilient.

Waste Reduction and Recycling

In the spirit of "leaving no trace," Barbados has implemented waste reduction and recycling programs. Hotels and businesses prioritize eco-friendly practices, reducing single-use plastics and encouraging responsible waste disposal. These efforts reflect Barbados' dedication to maintaining its pristine environment for both residents and visitors.

Barbados' approach to sustainable tourism is a harmonious dance between nature, culture, and responsible practices. By embracing these principles, the island not only offers an unforgettable experience for travelers but also sets an example for the global tourism industry.

CHAPTER EIGHT

Shopping In Barbados

Did you know that Barbados is also a shopper's paradise? With its blend of high-end luxury shopping and unique local goods, shopping in Barbados is an experience that cannot be missed.

One of the most popular shopping destinations in Barbados is the Limegrove Lifestyle Centre. This luxurious shopping complex is located in the heart of Holetown, one of the island's most exclusive neighborhoods. The Limegrove Lifestyle Centre is home to over 100 stores, ranging from high-end fashion brands like Louis Vuitton and Michael Kors, to local boutiques that offer handmade jewelry and crafts. With its sophisticated atmosphere and high-end amenities, the Limegrove Lifestyle Centre is a must-visit for anyone looking for luxury shopping in Barbados.

If you're looking for a more traditional shopping experience, head to Bridgetown, the island's capital city. Bridgetown is home to a variety of markets and shops that offer a unique look at local culture. The Pelican Village Craft Centre is a great place to start your shopping adventure in Bridgetown. This open-air market features over 20 shops that sell handmade crafts, textiles, and other souvenirs that are unique to Barbados. You'll find everything from pottery and ceramics to handmade clothing and accessories at Pelican Village, making it a great place to find gifts and souvenirs to take home with you.

For those looking for a more modern shopping experience, head to the Sheraton Mall in Christ Church. This shopping center is one of the largest on the island and offers a wide range of stores that cater to all types of shoppers. Whether you're looking for clothing, electronics, or home goods, you'll find it at the Sheraton Mall. And, with its convenient location near some of the island's best beaches, the Sheraton Mall is a great place to pick up some beachwear or accessories before hitting the sand.

If you're interested in exploring the local food scene, head to the Oistins Fish Market. This outdoor market is located in the town of Oistins and is a popular destination for both locals and tourists alike. Here, you'll find fresh seafood that has been caught that day, as well as a variety of other local foods like macaroni pie, plantains, and cou-cou. The Oistins Fish Market is a great place to sample some of the island's best cuisine while also experiencing the vibrant local culture.

Of course, no shopping trip to Barbados would be complete without a visit to the rum shops. Rum is a big part of the local culture in Barbados, and there are a variety of rum shops located throughout the island. These small bars and shops offer a relaxed atmosphere where locals and tourists alike can enjoy a cold drink and some good conversation. And, of course, you'll also have the opportunity to sample some of the island's best rum, which is made from the sugar cane that grows abundantly on the island.

Overall, shopping in Barbados is an experience that is not to be missed. From luxury shopping at the Limegrove Lifestyle Centre to exploring local markets and rum shops, there is something for every type of shopper on the island. And, with its stunning beaches, vibrant culture, and warm hospitality, Barbados is the perfect destination for a memorable shopping trip that you won't soon forget.

Local Markets And Shopping Malls

Local Markets

These markets not only provide a glimpse into the authentic Bajan way of life but also offer a diverse array of goods, from fresh produce and handicrafts to unique local delicacies. If you're a visitor looking to experience the heart of Barbados, be sure to add these local markets to your itinerary:

Cheapside Market: Located in Bridgetown, the capital city, Cheapside Market is a vibrant hub of activity. This bustling market is known for its fresh produce, including colorful tropical fruits, vegetables, herbs, and spices. It's a great place to interact with local farmers and vendors, and you can find everything from ripe mangoes to aromatic Bajan seasonings. Don't forget to try the famous Bajan hot sauce, a fiery condiment that's a staple in Barbadian cuisine.

Oistins Fish Market: For a taste of Barbados' rich maritime heritage, head to Oistins Fish Market on the south coast. This lively market is famous for its fresh seafood, particularly the Friday Night Fish Fry. Every Friday evening, locals and visitors gather to enjoy an outdoor feast featuring grilled and fried fish, lobster, shrimp, and other delights, all accompanied by live music and a festive atmosphere.

Hastings Farmers Market: If you're looking for a more relaxed market experience, the Hastings Farmers Market is a must-visit. Set in a picturesque courtyard, this market offers a charming selection of organic produce, locally made crafts, and artisanal goods. From handmade jewelry to natural skincare products, you'll find a range of unique souvenirs to take back home.

Pelican Craft Centre: Located in Bridgetown, the Pelican Craft Centre is a haven for arts and crafts enthusiasts. This market showcases the work of talented local artisans, offering handmade jewelry, pottery, wood carvings, and other traditional crafts. It's an ideal place to find one-of-a-kind souvenirs that capture the essence of Barbadian creativity.

Holders Farmers Market: For a mix of gourmet foods, artisanal products, and a dash of local entertainment, the Holders Farmers Market is a delightful choice. Held in the beautifully landscaped grounds of Holders House, this market features a range of offerings, from organic produce and gourmet cheeses to handcrafted chocolates and fine wines.

Bridgetown Market: For a truly immersive cultural experience, time your visit to coincide with the Bridgetown Market. Held during the Barbados Crop Over Festival, this lively event transforms the capital into a colorful extravaganza. You'll find a wide range of local foods, arts, and crafts, along with live music, parades, and energetic dance performances.

When exploring these local markets, remember to embrace the friendly spirit of Barbados and engage with the vendors and fellow visitors. Bargaining is not the norm in Barbadian markets, so approach your shopping with a respectful and appreciative attitude.

Shopping Malls

From high-end boutiques to charming artisan stalls, Barbados' shopping malls cater to every taste and preference. Let's take a closer look at some of the top shopping malls that are a must-visit for every visitor.

Limegrove Lifestyle Centre: Located in Holetown, Limegrove Lifestyle Centre is a premier shopping destination that effortlessly blends luxury with the laid-back Caribbean atmosphere. This open-air mall features a carefully curated selection of high-end boutiques offering fashion, accessories, jewelry, and cosmetics from renowned international brands. Limegrove also houses several art galleries, restaurants, and a state-of-the-art cinema for a complete entertainment experience.

Sheraton Mall: For a more diverse shopping experience that combines global brands with local flavor, the Sheraton Mall in Christ Church is an excellent choice. Visitors can explore a wide range of shops offering clothing, electronics, souvenirs, and more. The mall also hosts various events and entertainment activities, making it a popular spot for families and groups.

Sky Mall: Sky Mall, located in Haggatt Hall, welcomes visitors with a unique shopping atmosphere. This mall caters to both locals and tourists, offering a blend of familiar international brands and authentic Barbadian products. The mall's spacious layout and vibrant atmosphere make it a pleasant place to spend an afternoon exploring shops, dining at its restaurants, or even catching a live music performance.

Lanterns Mall: Situated in the bustling south coast of Barbados, Lanterns Mall is a charming shopping center that provides a mix of shopping, dining, and entertainment options. Visitors can enjoy a diverse selection of stores, ranging from fashion boutiques to specialty shops offering local crafts and gifts. The mall's central location makes it convenient for those looking to explore the vibrant nightlife of the St. Lawrence Gap area.

Bridgetown Cruise Terminal: If you're arriving by cruise ship, the Bridgetown Cruise Terminal offers a unique shopping experience right at the port. Here, you'll find duty-free shops selling a wide range of products, from luxury items to local souvenirs. It's a convenient stop for cruise passengers looking to pick up gifts or indulge in some retail therapy before continuing their journey.

Pelican Village Craft Centre: While not a traditional shopping mall, Pelican Village Craft Centre in Bridgetown is a must-visit for those seeking authentic Barbadian crafts and souvenirs. This vibrant artisan market showcases the work of local craftsmen, including pottery, artwork, jewelry, and textiles. Visitors can witness the creative process, engage with the artists, and take home one-of-a-kind mementos that reflect the island's culture.

Souvenirs And Gifts To Buy

A visit to Barbados is not only an opportunity to bask in its scenic beauty and vibrant culture but also a chance to bring back a piece of the island's charm through unique souvenirs and gifts. From handcrafted artistry to local delicacies, Barbados offers an array of items that encapsulate its rich heritage and make for unforgettable mementos. Here is a list of captivating souvenirs and gifts you should consider taking home from your Barbadian adventure.

Bajan Rum: Barbados is known as the birthplace of rum, and a bottle of locally-produced Bajan rum is a quintessential souvenir. Choose from a variety of brands and flavors, including the world-renowned Mount Gay Rum. Some distilleries also offer guided tours that provide insight into the rum-making process, making the experience even more memorable.

Art and Crafts: Barbados is teeming with artistic talent, and purchasing local art and crafts is a wonderful way to support the island's creative community. Look for vibrant paintings, intricate pottery, and beautifully woven baskets that reflect the island's culture and natural beauty. Places like Pelican Village Craft Centre in Bridgetown are great for discovering unique handmade items.

Mahogany Creations: Barbados is known for its exquisite mahogany woodwork. You'll find a variety of items crafted from this rich wood, including jewelry, sculptures, and furniture. These items showcase the skilled craftsmanship and attention to detail that make them truly exceptional gifts or keepsakes.

Bajan Hot Sauce and Seasonings: For food enthusiasts, Bajan hot sauces and seasonings are a must-buy. These locally-made condiments often feature fiery flavors and unique combinations of spices that add a touch of Barbadian zest to your dishes back home. These make for flavorful and practical gifts that encapsulate the island's culinary heritage.

Sea Island Cotton Products: Barbados is home to Sea Island Cotton, a rare and luxurious type of cotton known for its softness and durability. Look for clothing, linens, and accessories made from this high-quality material, offering both comfort and elegance. These products are a true embodiment of Barbados' dedication to quality.

Bajan Black Cake: Black Cake is a traditional Barbadian dessert that's a favorite during festive occasions. Made with rich ingredients like dried fruits and rum, this cake has a distinct flavor that's worth savoring. Consider bringing back a boxed Black Cake mix or a pre-made cake to share the island's culinary delight with your loved ones.

Local Artisan Jewelry: Barbados boasts an array of skilled jewelry artisans who create stunning pieces inspired by the island's natural beauty. Look for unique designs featuring precious and semi-precious stones, corals, and shells, capturing the essence of the Caribbean in wearable art.

Essential Websites And Apps For Travelers

From finding the best local attractions to staying connected and informed, here's a detailed list of websites and apps that will be indispensable for travelers visiting Barbados:

1. Visit Barbados Official Website (https://www.visitbarbados.org/): The official tourism website of Barbados is a comprehensive resource for planning your trip. It offers information on accommodations, activities, events, and attractions across the island. You can also find travel tips, suggested itineraries, and insights into local culture and cuisine.

2. Google Maps (Website: https://www.google.com/maps; App: Google Maps): Google Maps is an essential tool for navigating Barbados. Use it to find directions, locate attractions, restaurants, and accommodations, and even explore the island's streets using Street View. Download offline maps to ensure you can navigate even without a stable internet connection.

3. Bajan Bus App (App: Bajan Bus): This app provides real-time bus schedules and routes for the public transportation system in Barbados. It's particularly useful for budget-conscious travelers looking to explore the island using local buses. The app helps you plan your route and estimate arrival times.

4. Barbados Yellow Pages (Website: https://www.findyello.com/barbados; App: Barbados Yellow Pages): For local businesses, services, and contact information, the Barbados Yellow Pages website and app are incredibly handy. Whether you're looking for restaurants, shops, or tour operators, this resource can help you find what you need.

5. WhatsApp (Website: https://www.whatsapp.com/; App: WhatsApp): WhatsApp is widely used in Barbados for communication. It's a great way to stay in touch with locals, fellow travelers, and even tour operators. It's also useful for making calls and sending messages over Wi-Fi, helping you save on international roaming charges.

6. Barbados Weather Apps (Apps: Various weather apps): Since weather can play a significant role in your travel plans, having a reliable weather app can be crucial. Apps like AccuWeather, The Weather Channel, or BBC Weather can help you stay updated on current conditions and forecasts in Barbados.

7. Moovit (Website: https://www.moovit.com/; App: Moovit): Moovit is a useful app for navigating the island's public transportation system. It provides real-time bus and train schedules, route planning, and notifications about service disruptions or delays.

8. ZIZOO (Website: https://www.zizoo.com/; App: ZIZOO): If you're interested in exploring Barbados by sea, ZIZOO is a platform that connects you with boat rentals and charter services. You can rent sailboats, catamarans, and yachts for a unique perspective of the island.

9. Currency Converter Apps (Apps: Various currency converter apps): To keep track of expenses and manage your budget, currency converter apps like XE Currency or OANDA Currency Converter are valuable tools. They help you convert Barbadian dollars (BBD) to your home currency accurately.

10. Social Media Apps (Apps: Facebook, Instagram, Twitter): Following local businesses, attractions, and official tourism accounts on social media can provide real-time updates, special offers, and insights into what's happening on the island during your visit.

These websites and apps will undoubtedly enhance your travel experience in Barbados by providing valuable information, guidance, and connectivity.

Travel Agencies And Tour Operators In Barbados

Exploring the stunning landscapes, vibrant culture, and unique experiences that Barbados has to offer becomes even more enjoyable with the assistance of local travel agencies and tour operators. These professionals are well-equipped to help you navigate the island's attractions, plan activities, and create memorable moments during your visit. Here's a list to some of the notable travel agencies and tour operators in Barbados:

1. SunTours Barbados (Website: https://www.suntoursbarbados.com/): SunTours Barbados is a well-established travel agency offering a wide range of tours and services, including island tours, water sports, private tours, and transportation services. With a reputation for excellent customer service, SunTours can help you tailor your experiences to your preferences.

2. Island Safari Barbados (Website: https://www.islandsafari.bb/): For those seeking a more adventurous exploration of Barbados, Island Safari offers exhilarating off-road tours through the island's rugged interior. These tours provide a unique opportunity to discover the island's natural beauty, wildlife, and culture in 4x4 vehicles.

3. Glory Tours (Website: https://www.glorytours.org/): Glory Tours specializes in personalized island tours, private transfers, and cruise ship excursions. Their knowledgeable guides offer insights into local history, culture, and attractions, ensuring an enriching experience for every traveler.

4. **Elegance Tours (Website: https://www.elegancetours.com/):** Elegance Tours focuses on providing customized private tours that allow you to explore Barbados at your own pace. From historical sites to scenic wonders, their guides ensure you get an in-depth understanding of the island's heritage.

5. **Cool Runnings Catamaran Cruises (Website: https://www.coolrunningsbarbados.com/):** For those looking to experience the turquoise waters surrounding Barbados, Cool Runnings offers catamaran cruises that include snorkeling, swimming with sea turtles, and enjoying a relaxing day at sea.

6. **Atlantis Submarines Barbados (Website: https://barbados.atlantissubmarines.com/):** For a unique underwater adventure, Atlantis Submarines offers submarine tours that allow you to explore Barbados' marine life and shipwrecks without getting wet. It's a fascinating experience for all ages.

7. **Oistins Fish Fry Tours (Website: https://www.oistinsfry.com/):** Oistins Fish Fry Tours focus on providing an authentic Barbadian experience by guiding you through the island's famous Friday night fish fry in Oistins. This bustling event is a must-visit for local food, music, and culture.

8. **Barbados Blue Watersports (Website: https://www.barbadosbluewatersports.com/):** For water enthusiasts, Barbados Blue Watersports offers a variety of activities, including snorkeling, paddleboarding, kayaking, and jet skiing. They provide both equipment rental and guided tours.

9. **Caribbean Safari Barbados (Website: http://www.caribbeansafari.bb/):** Caribbean Safari offers guided tours through Barbados' natural landscapes, including its lush

countryside and historic landmarks. Their knowledgeable guides share stories about the island's history, flora, and fauna.

10. SunTours Car Rentals (Website: https://www.suntourscarrentals.com/): If you prefer to explore Barbados at your own pace, SunTours Car Rentals provides reliable rental vehicles that allow you to independently discover the island's hidden gems.

These are just a few examples of the travel agencies and tour operators available in Barbados.

Glossary Of Common Bajan Terms For Visitors

Bajan: A term used to refer to the people or things from Barbados.

Lime: To hang out or socialize with friends.

Breadfruit: A starchy fruit commonly used in Barbadian cuisine.

Conkie: A traditional Barbadian dish made from cornmeal, coconut, and sweet potatoes, typically wrapped in banana leaves.

Cutters: Sandwiches made with various fillings, often enjoyed at local food stalls.

Coupé: A type of local minibus used for public transportation.

Zafrina: A sweet drink made from hibiscus flowers.

Wukking up: A lively and energetic style of dancing.

De ting sweet: Referring to something that is enjoyable or pleasing.

Auntie/Uncle: Terms of respect used to address older individuals.

Maco: Someone who gossips or is overly curious about others' affairs.

Sweet bread: A type of cake made with dried fruits and spices.

Backra: Historically used to refer to white slave masters; now used more generally to mean any authority figure.

Fishcakes: Deep-fried snacks made from seasoned fish and dough.

Bajan pepper sauce: Spicy sauce made from local peppers.

Chupse: An expression of disagreement or disdain.

Banks Beer: The locally brewed beer in Barbados.

Oistins: A fishing village famous for its Friday night fish fry.

Mudda: Slang for mother.

Dub: To ignore or not pay attention to something.

Soupie: A term used for someone who is inquisitive.

Hillaby: A hilly area in central Barbados.

Crop Over: An annual festival celebrating the end of the sugarcane harvest season.

Hot-steppin': Walking quickly or confidently.

Swank: Dressing stylishly.

Pot fish: Cooking fish with vegetables in a pot.

Ram goat: Goat meat cooked in various ways, a traditional dish.

Rack of lamb: A popular dish often served with Bajan seasoning.

Bajan blackbelly sheep: A breed of sheep native to Barbados.

Flying fish cutter: A sandwich made with flying fish.

Sea egg: A sea urchin, often enjoyed as a delicacy.

Bajan macaroni pie: A baked pasta dish similar to mac and cheese.

Cheese on bread: An expression of surprise or frustration.

Gully: A small valley or ravine.

Cawmere: Colloquial term for Queen's College, a prominent school in Barbados.

Green lime: Unripe or sour lime, used in cooking.

Bigging up: Praising or complimenting someone.

Nuff: A lot or plenty.

On a shoestring: Managing with very little money.

Duggering: Eavesdropping or being overly attentive.

Gyaff: Chatting or talking aimlessly.

Head hard: Stubborn or hard-headed.

Kaiso: A style of Barbadian calypso music.

Cricket: A popular sport in Barbados.

Soup kitchen: A local food establishment serving traditional soups.

Fête: A lively and enjoyable party or event.

Juck: To poke or stab.

Landship: A traditional Barbadian organization with historical roots.

Mashup: Ruined or destroyed.

Mout' cut: When someone says something disrespectful or offensive.

Fuh real: Absolutely true or sincere.

Plantation: Historical estates often associated with sugar production.

Peel head: A bald person.

Braggot: A traditional Bajan drink made from beer and honey.

Souse: A dish made from pickled pork, often served with breadfruit or sweet potato.

Sweet mauby: A refreshing drink made from the bark of the mauby tree.

Sun hot: The weather is hot.

Pudding and souse: A dish of pickled pork and sweet potato.

Rice 'n' peas: A dish made from rice and pigeon peas.

Two-left-foot: Clumsy or uncoordinated.

Mout' 'fraid: Afraid to speak one's mind.

Bragging rights: Having the right to boast or brag about something.

Collins: A popular Bajan cocktail made from lemon, sugar, and soda water.

Gully-washer: A heavy rainstorm.

Pig-tail soup: A soup made with smoked pig tails and various vegetables.

In de dog house: In trouble or facing displeasure.

Mauby: A traditional drink made from the bark of the mauby tree.

Suck teeth: An expression of annoyance or disapproval made by sucking air through one's teeth.

T'ing: Slang for "thing," often used informally.

X mark: A term used for a kiss (e.g., "send meh a x mark").

Remember that the Bajan dialect can be colorful and rich with cultural context. Using some of these terms might help you better connect with locals and immerse yourself in the island's vibrant culture.

CONCLUSION

Waving Farewell To The Soul Of The Caribbean

As your journey through the pages of this travel guide to Barbados comes to a close, I hope you find yourself standing at the crossroads of reality and memory, carrying with you the echoes of crashing waves, the whispers of swaying palms, and the warmth of the sun's embrace. The enchantment of Barbados lies not merely in its pristine beaches and vibrant landscapes, but in the profound connection it forges with each traveler fortunate enough to grace its shores.

As you bid farewell to this guide, remember that Barbados is more than a destination; it's an experience that weaves itself into the very fabric of your soul. The stories you've collected along its rugged coasts, in the bustling markets, and amidst the melodies of its vibrant culture are now etched into the tapestry of your life's adventures.

From the breathtaking vistas of Harrison's Cave to the laughter-filled nights of Oistins Fish Fry, you've embraced the rhythm of this island with an open heart. You've tasted the flavors of its cuisine, both in the exquisite delicacies and the humble street food, each bite a tribute to the passion of its people.

As you reflect on the moments shared with locals, whether while liming under the shade of a tree or discovering the history within the walls of Bridgetown, remember that you've become a part of this mosaic, leaving your footprints in the sand as a testament to the beauty of exploration and the unity of cultures.

The island's vibrant festivals and warm-hearted people have embraced you, inviting you to dance, to celebrate, and to simply be. It's a place where time slows down, where laughter fills the air, and where the whispers of the past are ever-present reminders of the resilience and spirit that define this nation.

As you close this guide, the spirit of Barbados lives on within you—a whisper of adventure, a taste of camaraderie, and a touch of wonder. Cherish the memories, relive the moments, and let the magic of Barbados linger in your heart, inspiring you to embark on future journeys with the same curiosity and open-heartedness that brought you here.

So, as the waves continue to kiss the shore and the sun dips below the horizon, remember that Barbados remains not just a destination, but a cherished chapter in the story of your life's exploration. Until we meet again on these golden sands or within the vibrant tapestry of your memories, may your heart forever be warmed by the sun, the sea, and the spirit of this beautiful island. Safe travels, dear wanderer, and may your adventures continue to unfold in the embrace of the world's wonders.

Made in the USA
Las Vegas, NV
13 October 2023